ℋISTORIC
TOURS
of OHIO

ℋISTORIC
TOURS
of OHIO

GARY S. WILLIAMS

GATEWAY PRESS, INC
Baltimore, MD   2007

Photos by Owen Williams
Cover Design by Kate Boyer

Please direct all correspondence and book orders to:
Gary S. Williams
42100 Williams Lane
Caldwell, OH 43724
Phone: (740) 732-8169 or (740) 732-7291
email: buckeye_books@earthlink.net
www.buckeyebookpress.com

Library of Congress Control Number 2007922015
ISBN: 978-0-9703395-3-9

Published for Buckeye Book Press by
Gateway Press, Inc.
3600 Clipper Mill Road, Suite 260
Baltimore, MD 21211-1953

Printed in the United States of America

Table of Contents

Introduction

The purpose of this book is to serve as a field guide to Ohio heritage tourism. The attractions described here are grouped topically and chronologically rather than geographically, so this is a tour guide only in the loosest sense. And for each site, more is discussed about the person or events connected to it than the contents of the site. This guidebook is meant to be consulted in preparation for a field trip to the places discussed to enhance appreciation of historical travel by giving background information on the topic.

All of these 100 plus sites have hours that are changing, and in far too many cases these changes are a reduction of hours. Some are open by appointment only. For this reason, hours and fees are not mentioned for the various sites and the reader is encouraged to contact the site before visiting. To assist in finding current information, the account for each entry in this book gives the following: mailing address, physical address (if different), telephone number and toll free number, if available, and website address.

There are many interesting Ohio people or places that are not included because there is not currently a museum or location devoted to the topic. The sites that are included here are by no means comprehensive, nor can they be labeled as the best. They are selected because they fit the categories for the book, and while they are all recommended, so are the many Ohio historical sites not included for profile here. The categories for this book are arranged to give an overview of Ohio history and also place it within the context of U.S. history. Each chapter covers a different time period as well as topic and they fall together as a whole, although each chapter can also be addressed individually by enthusiasts of certain subjects.

The book begins with a discussion of the ancient mound builders and the works they left behind in Ohio. Within one hundred years of their first contact with English speaking white men the last Native Americans left Ohio, and chapter two focuses on the period of white and Indian interaction on the Ohio frontier. Chapter three concentrates on the role Ohio played in the Underground Railroad and chapter four tells of the Ohio-reared generals who won the Civil War after the slavery issue erupted into war. Four Ohio-born Civil War generals went on to become President, and chapter five focuses on the seven Presidents born in Ohio who served in a 55-year period. Chapter six concentrates on authors and inventors/scientists who had Ohio connections.

A final chapter addresses the omission of many fine museums and sites that did not fit into the previous chapters, and attempts to include them in additional categories. In all, there are over 100 sites in 55 different counties for which contact information is offered. There is also a bibliography for further reading on specialized Ohio topics and the index has all sites arranged by county with the page number where contact information can be found.

It is surprising how many prominent Ohioans knew each other, and in cases where discussion of one site involves another, a cross reference with page number is provided. This helps illustrate the interconnected nature of history to show the relationships between people in an era and in the flow of national history. And in doing so, this guide also hopes to enable students and history buffs to plan a one-tank trip into the state's storied past.

Acknowledgments

As always, the immediate family bears the brunt of support for a book project. I have been lucky in that my wife Mary Williams has always encouraged me in all literary endeavors. In addition, our son Owen Williams was responsible for all illustrations, layout and design and our daughter Meryl Williams typed the manuscript.

Proofreading and suggestions came from Miriam Marcosson, Les Williams and Roger Pickenpaugh. Bill Hanner provided photographs and suggestions, and Brian Williams offered photos and extensive editing help. Advice for specific chapters came from Cathy Nelson of the Ohio Friends of Freedom Society and Tom Wolf of the Ohio Historical Society.

And finally, I would like to thank all of the employees and volunteers at all the historic sites in Ohio for all the time they devote to interpreting our past.

Chapter One:
The Mound Builders

It is easy to study the history of Ohio when the makers of history leave extensive documentation behind. But the state's prehistory can be unearthed only by archeology. For the vast period before the arrival of white men late in the 17th century, the lack of written records means that physical artifacts are our only source of information. Yet there is still a wealth of such findings that give a tantalizing glimpse of the mysteries of pre-historic Ohio.

From some of the state's excavation sites it has been determined that Paleo-Indians were battling mastodons here as long as 10,000 years ago. And we now know that more recently, a mere 2,000 years ago, that a prehistoric culture that was the center of a vast trading network flourished here. Clues left behind by the Adena and Hopewell cultures give indication of a successful and peaceful native culture that was centered in what is now southern Ohio, although without records it is impossible to pinpoint exact dates and details.

We do know that these cultures emerged during the Woodland Period, which ran roughly from 1000 B.C. to 1000 A.D. The cultures of this era were characterized by limited farming, pottery, trade, and mortuary practices that involved burial away from living areas. In the early Woodland Period, a group that scientists call the Glacial Kame people arrived in what is now Ohio. These people were known to bury their dead in natural mounds and sometimes practiced cremation or staining of the body.

They were followed by the Adena culture, which flourished in the Ohio River watershed between Pittsburgh and Louisville from around 1000 B.C. to 100 A.D. The Adena actually buried their more prominent members in mounds that were not unlike the pyramids, and the remains of these mounds can be found all over southern Ohio. The Adena built their mounds in visible spots near streams but on terraces that were well above the normal floodplain. And, as in the pyramids, the deceased were buried with grave goods, or possessions they had accumulated in their lifetime. But the Adena mounds contained multiple burials in a diversity of styles and locations. The more elaborate tombs involved wooden buildings called charnel houses that were used to prepare the body and then collapsed or buried around it. Many of the Adena mounds were also added on to over a period of time, and some of the ones that became quite large were surrounded by a ditch or moat.

The Adena were supplanted by the Hopewell culture, which flourished between 200 B.C. and 500 A.D., and centered its activities in the same area. There is no way to be sure that the Hopewell descended from the Adena, so slight differences in their practices has resulted in their being labeled a separate culture. The Hopewell had more complex mortuary procedures and more advanced earthworks than the Adena. In addition to burial mounds, the Hopewell also built complex geometric earthworks and hilltop enclosures.

The Hopewell lived in small, scattered villages but gathered at these centralized earthworks for special ceremonial and religious occasions. They seem to have been a peaceful and egalitarian people, with little evidence of military strife or aggressive leadership. Yet they also were involved in an extensive trade network that would seem to in-

2

dicate a prosperous and successful civilization. The grave goods found in their tombs include such diverse items as shells and sharks teeth from the Gulf Coast, obsidian and grizzly teeth from the Rockies, and copper from Lake Superior.

Like any society, their success was at least in part determined by the natural resources of the lands they inhabited. The Hopewell clearly were favored in this area. Licking County has an extensive outcropping of flint that was useful in fashioning essential stone tools. And along the Ohio River were large deposits of pipestone that was used to sculpt effigy pipes that became the most fascinating artifacts that the Hopewell left behind. The Hopewell were so dependent on these resources that some speculate that they built a road system connecting these sites to their spiritual center around Chillicothe.

The Hopewell also were sophisticated enough to have some understanding of astronomy. At some of their geometric earthworks the alignment of certain features are in conjunction with celestial events. As an agrarian people, it would be important for them to have an understanding of the calendar for planting purposes, but the astronomical events may also have had a spiritual connection.

We do not know if the Hopewell died out, moved on, or successfully evolved into something else. A culture referred to as the Intrusive Mound People used the existing mounds to bury their dead between 700 and 1000 A.D., but little is known about these people. More is known about the Fort Ancient culture, a late Woodland group that prospered from about 1000 A.D. until shortly before the arrival of Europeans. These people were more involved in agriculture and cultivated crops like maize. They also lived in palisaded villages and in addition to burial mounds, they also built effigy mounds in the shape of various animals. Although they lived in the same places as the Adena and Hopewell, it is one of many ancient mysteries whether they were descendents of these people. Equally interesting is the notion that the Fort Ancient may have been the ancestors of tribes such as the Shawnee, who were here when the white men arrived.

When settlers began moving here in the late 18th century, neither they nor the current native inhabitants knew anything about the various mounds dotting the landscape. With some exceptions, the whites developed the prime land that the mounds had been built on, often obliterating all traces. But there was considerable curiosity about the remains that were still visible. The first study of the mounds was published in 1820 by Caleb Atwater of Circleville, a town that had been named for the mound it was built on.

In 1833, Daniel Webster attended graduation ceremonies at Kenyon College and offered encouragement to scholar Edwin Davis, who had given an oration on the Antiquities of Ohio. Davis became a physician in Chillicothe and shared his enthusiasm with George Squier, the editor of the *Chillicothe Gazette*. The pair studied mounds extensively and in 1848 collaborated to produce *Ancient Monuments of the Mississippi Valley*, which was the first scientific publication of the newly established Smithsonian Institution. This groundbreaking study included detailed maps and drawings that are still useful today, especially since erosion and development have erased even more of the mounds. Unfortunately, Squier and Davis had a falling out, and Davis wound up selling their accumulated artifacts to an English collector located in Salisbury, ironically just a few miles from Stonehenge. Today this collection is housed in the British Museum in London.

4

Scientists continued to be interested in Ohio's mounds. Archeologists Frederick Ward Putnam and Warren Moorehead unearthed artifacts for display in Chicago's World Columbian Exposition of 1893 that kept up interest and helped with preservation efforts. After 1900, the state of Ohio became involved, and excavation under William Mills and Henry Shetrone furthered these efforts.

New discoveries are still being made about these sites today, as recent revelations about Serpent Mound have greatly altered what we thought we knew. And emerging theories concern connections between mound sites and possible astronomical functions. Some of Ohio's best sites for observing ancient cultures are now state or federal parks with museums on the grounds. Here are some of them.

Serpent Mound State Memorial

Probably the most famous ancient Indian earthwork in Ohio is Serpent Mound in Adams County. This unique feature has been variously interpreted by many schools of thought and has something to offer them all in its mysteries. In the 19th century, some Christian ministers considered it evidence that the Garden of Eden had been located in Ohio and the serpent had been left as a marker. More recently, New Age believers in a nature-centered worship have flocked here to celebrate harmonic convergence and a link to ancient peoples. Those of a more scientific bent have marveled at the mound's alignment with astronomical events at certain times of the year, which shows an understanding of geometry and astronomy not expected of a non-literate culture. And the fact that Serpent Mound is built upon a type of rock not found anywhere else nearby even gives the alien theorists some food for thought. As an archeological wonder, it is Ohio's Stonehenge.

What is known for certain about Serpent Mound is that at 1,348 feet, or just over a quarter mile, it is the longest effigy mound in North America. It is also one of only two remaining Ohio mounds built in the shape of an animal, the other being Alligator Mound near Granville in Licking County. But what we know about Serpent Mound is subject to change. At one time it was believed to be thousands of years old, but recent testing has shown it to be "only" a thousand years old, and one of the more recent sites built by the Fort Ancient culture. This discovery has sparked speculation that the site may represent a sort of missing link between ancient Indians and the tribesmen encountered by European intruders a few centuries later, as the Shawnee tribe was known to have been in Ohio early on and the serpent played a role in Shawnee mythology.

Serpent Mound lies on a plateau 100 feet above Ohio Brush Creek. The unique rock on the site is believed to have come from an underground gas explosion thousands of years ago. Nearby the serpent are three Adena type conical burial mounds, but the more recent unique serpent effigy is the main attraction. The earthwork depicts a wriggling snake with an open mouth that is about to swallow a large oval. It was built by laying out stones in a pattern and then covering them first with yellow clay and then soil. The mound was built to a height of four to five feet and is twenty feet across at the base.

While other details about the design and purpose of Serpent Mound are unknown, the story of how the site came to be preserved is well known. In 1887, the site was excavated by Frederick Ward Putnam, Curator of Archeology and Ethnology at Harvard's Peabody Museum. Putnam displayed artifacts from Serpent Mound at the World's Columbia Exposition in 1893, which did much to raise awareness of North American antiquities. To prevent Serpent Mound from being lost to development, Putnam raised $6,000 to purchase the site for Harvard. The University deeded the property to the state of Ohio in 1900 with the stipulation that there be public access. The state was agreeable to this, as in 1888, the legislature had passed the nation's first state law for protection of archeological sites.

Today the Serpent Mound State Memorial is administered by the Ohio Historical Society. Also on the grounds is a museum open in summer months, while the site and public restrooms are accessible year round during daylight hours. There is a paved trail that encircles the serpent and side trails that go down to Ohio Brush Creek. A special feature is a 25-foot tower that gives an overview of the layout of the earthwork. Serpent Mound is located just off State Route 41, four miles west of the junction of State Route 73. To find current information on current hours or fees, write to: Serpent Mound State Memorial, 3850 SR 73, Peebles, 45660-9221, or call 937-587-2796, or 800-752-2787. Additional information can be accessed at *www.ohiohistory.org/places/serpent/*.

Hopewell Culture National Historical Park

The city of Chillicothe was founded in 1796 and just seven years later became the capital of the new state of Ohio. But the Chillicothe area was a "capital" of sorts around 1,500 years earlier, when it was at the heart of a Hopewell culture whose trading network spanned the continent. The Hopewell were not a political or military empire and had no known capital as such, but their ceremonial life was centered in present-day Ross County, which features the most numerous and diverse of North American earthworks.

Among the many sites clustered around the Scioto River are two that gave their names to the two most predominant ancient cultures. Williams Mills of the Ohio Archeological and Historical Society did an excavation of a mound near Thomas Worthington's stone mansion Adena, and Mills gave this name to the Indian culture he was investigating. It was here in 1901 that he found the Adena pipe, an eight-inch tall effigy pipe of a dwarf. The artifacts of a culture determined to have flourished slightly later were found in the nearby farm of Mordecai Hopewell, and his name is used to describe them. The periods of these two cultures overlapped in Ohio and it's entirely possible the Hopewell were more advanced descendents of the Adena, but for archeological purposes, they are defined as separate cultures.

Many mound sites of the Chillicothe area have been lost to development, and some, such as the original Adena mound, are no longer accessible to the public. But some of the best have been preserved as part of the Hopewell Culture National Historical Park. Headquartered near two prisons on State Route 104 just north of Route 35, this park along the Scioto features a sixteen-acre embankment and burial mound complex that includes 23 separate mounds.

Some of this site was damaged during World War I when the area was called Camp Sherman and used for military training. But in 1923, the federal government took stewardship and made the Mound City Group a national monument. In 1992 the site was upgraded to national historic park status and given its current name. The site now features a museum and visitor's center that is open year round every day but holidays. Visitors can walk around the perimeter and among the mounds. Most prominent is the central mound, where the remains of seventeen natives were found, and the remains of the Mound of the Pipes, where nearly 200 pipes made of Ohio pipestone were unearthed. Many of these and other artistic efforts are on display in the museum.

The National Park Service also administers several other mounds in the area. Among the most notable of these is Seip Mound, seventeen miles west of Chillicothe on Route 50. The remains of 122 people were unearthed on this site, which is marked by a roadside rest area today. To find out more, contact the Hopewell Culture Memorial Historic Park at 16062 St. Rt. 104, Chillicothe, 45601-9701 or call 740-774-1125, or go to *www.nps.gov/hocu/index.htm.*

Flint Ridge State Memorial

The ancient Hopewell culture had such a vast trading network in the first few centuries A.D. that their partners were all over North America. For a people to have such an extensive commercial network, they had to have had some sort of advantage in terms of natural resources. A main basis for their prosperity was Flint Ridge, one of the best and largest deposits of quality flint in the eastern United States.

The deposits here are as thick as twelve feet and are available in many different colors. This flint was ideal for fashioning primitive tools, and for the Hopewell to have access to the site would be equivalent today to sitting on top of significant petroleum deposits. Much of the rock is above the surface, but the best flint had to be quarried from underground and split off in wedges with crude tools. Flint Ridge served as a factory for production of this needed resource.

10

The remains of large quarry pits are still visible on the wind-swept ridge today, some as large as twenty feet deep and 60 feet in diameter, just a few miles away from busy Interstate 70. Flint Ridge State Memorial is a 525-acre preserve, established in 1933. A museum was built over one of the larger quarry pits in 1968 and was renovated in 1999. The museum is open in the summer months and the site is open year round in daylight hours.

There are three nature trails that go through the woods past several quarry sites. A unique feature is a handicap access trail, a paved path with a guide rope and interpretive signs posted in Braille. While it is prohibited to remove flint from the site, amateur geologists can delight in the rock outcroppings that have been of interest to man for thousands of years.

Flint Ridge State Memorial is in Licking County on County Road 668, a few miles north of the Brownsville exit of I-70. For information about hours and costs, contact Flint

Ridge State Memorial, 7091 Brownsville RD SE, Glenford, 43739-9609, or call 740-787-2476, or 800-283-8707 or go to *www.ohiohistory.org/places/flint/.*

Moundbuilders State Memorial and Octagon State Memorial

The presence of rock deposits at Flint Ridge made the area an important locale for the ancient Indians, and there are about a dozen mounds and earthworks found in Licking County. The most significant of these are the Great Circle and Octagon earthworks located in the western part of the city of Newark. They are a part of what is considered the largest set of geometric earthworks known and are assumed to have religious and ceremonial significance. This Hopewell site was spread over a four-mile area and is now accessible at two places.

The Great Circle earthworks, called Moundbuilders State Memorial, is located just off State Route 79, north of Heath, and also has a parking area at 21st and Cooper Streets. This mound is a circle 1,200 feet in diameter that encloses an area covering twenty acres. The walls are from eight to fourteen feet high, and the circle is surrounded by a ditch. There are four smaller mounds inside the circle and one large opening in the circle walls. Near the opening the state built a museum in 1971 that was the first museum in the United States dedicated completely to prehistoric Native American art. The museum is open in the summer months, but the site is accessible year round during daylight hours.

Raised paths lead from Great Circle mound and portions of them are visible nearby. They connected this spot to Octagon State Memorial, which is located off 33rd Street, north of Main Street. This site, which covers 120 acres, consists of a circle connected by two earth walls to an octagon. The city of Newark leased the site to a golf course in 1910 before deeding the property to the state in 1933. This has resulted in a state memorial that is shared with Moundbuilders Country Club. While access is limited during golf times, the site can be viewed from a trail along part of the circle and a raised platform located near where the circle and octagon are connected. Other Hopewell sites featured a similar circle and octagon pattern, but the significance of this eludes us today.

All eight points of the octagon have openings that can be walked through but are blocked by smaller mounds that obstruct outsiders from seeing inside. Recent research indicates that the primitive Hopewell may have had a sophisticated knowledge of geometry and astronomy. A mound eight feet higher than the rest of the circle wall is at the part of the circle directly opposite the pathway connecting to the octagon. By standing on this mound and looking through the path through the octagon, the view lines up with the northernmost point of where the moon rises on the eastern horizon as it fluctuates over a complex 18.6-year cycle. The Hopewell figured this out, which means that the site was built over a period of time and that they were capable of calculations beyond what is normally thought of ancient cultures.

Another intriguing aspect of the Newark Earthworks is the long stretches of parallel walls that lead from them. Early maps indicated that these routes extended for several miles before fading out into developed lands. Archaeologist Bradley Lepper of the Ohio Historical Society has determined that these walls, if extended, would lead directly towards Chillicothe. Lepper speculates that this may have been part of a Great Hopewell Road that connected the principle Hopewell ceremonial centers. This route would have been built around the same time that the Mayan culture was building more famous straight roads.

For information about the Newark Earthworks, contact Moundbuilders State Memorial, 99 Cooper Avenue, Newark, 43055-2422, or call either 740-344-1919 or 800-600-7178. Information can also be found on *www.ohiohistory.org/places/newarkearthworks/*.

Fort Hill State Memorial

In addition to burial mounds and geometric earthworks, the Hopewell also built hilltop enclosures along natural ridges. These structures are called forts, but their purpose seems to have been for ceremonial gatherings rather than defense. One of the best examples of this is Fort Hill in eastern Highland County, located off State Route 41, just south of Cynthiana. The enclosure at Fort Hill is 400 feet above the flood plain of Ohio Brush Creek. The outline of the fort follows the contours of the ridge top with a perimeter of 1.6 miles, enclosing some 40 acres. The walls built along this ridge top range from six to fifteen feet high and are 40 to 45 feet wide. There are 33 openings in the fort's walls, each one about twenty feet wide. But the work blends in so well with the surroundings that it is difficult to tell that it is man-made.

Fort Hill was built in stages over a long period of time. The builders first outlined the perimeter with stones and subsoil that were already there. Then they covered this with large slabs of quarried sandstone. A stone retaining wall was later added to the inside of the wall, and then covered with more soil and rock. It was clearly a major construction effort to haul rocks to such a remote location, and there is evidence of possible dormitories for workers on the site.

Today, Fort Hill State Memorial is a 1,200-acre park that has been designated a natural preserve, and features a wide diversity of plants and trees. There are ten miles of hiking trails available that skirt the base and go up to the top. A museum opened on the grounds in 2001 focuses on the area's natural history and geology as well as Hopewell archaeology. The museum is open only in summer, but the grounds are accessible year round during daylight hours. For more information, contact Fort Hill State Memorial, 13614 Fort Hill Road, Cynthiana, 45133-9033, or call 513-588-3221, or 800-283-8905. Information can also be found at *www.ohiohistory.org/places/fthill/*.

15

Fort Ancient State Memorial

Fort Ancient has been one of Ohio's best-known Indian sites since it was named Ohio's first state park in 1891. But this irregular shaped hilltop enclosure goes back much further than that. Archaeologists now believe that the Hopewell built this earthwork in two phases, with the southern half being done first, and the narrow connecting part and northern portion added later.

The finished product that stands on a ridge 275 feet above the Little Miami River has a perimeter of 3.5 miles and encloses 125 acres. The walls of the fort range from four to twenty-three feet in height, depending on exterior terrain. The walls are higher where the hill is less steep, and lower where not needed due to the steeper hillsides. Inside the walls are several mounds and 67 U-shaped gateways that obstruct the view from outside, but do not bar entrance. While remains of wood structures have been found within the fort, archaeologists believe that the site was never occupied by residents but used only for special gatherings. These functions may have been religious or political, and alignment of the mounds inside indicates a possible astronomic function as well.

Unfortunately for historical clarity, Fort Ancient was not built by the Fort Ancient people, although it was later used by them. The term "Fort Ancient Culture" was used in 1893 when archaeologists were uncovering artifacts for display in the Columbian Expositions. But it turns out the experts were off by about a millennium, as the site was actually built by the Hopewell between 100 B.C. and 300 A.D. It was

16

around 1000 A.D. that the Fort Ancient people occupied the existing site and set up a palisaded village and began growing crops here. These later Fort Ancient people may be a missing link to the Indian tribes who were in Ohio when white men arrived, but even less is known about the connection between the Hopewell and the Fort Ancient cultures.

There is enough intriguing connection that today the Ohio Historical Society has designated Fort Ancient as the Gateway site to American Indian Heritage. In 1998 a museum was opened that features 9,000 square feet of exhibit space. A unique feature on the grounds is a garden devoted to plants cultivated by the ancient natives. Located in Warren County between exits 32 and 36 of I-71, Fort Ancient can be found by following signs from each exit. The grounds are open daily, while the museum hours are seasonal. For more information concerning hours and costs, contact Fort Ancient State Memorial, 6123 St. Rt. 350, Oregonia, 45054-9708, or call 513-932-4421, or 800-283-8904. Information can also be found at *www.ohiohistory.org/places/ftancien/*.

Other Mounds

There are nearly sixty documented earthworks and mounds in Ohio, only a handful of which have museums on the site. But there are several mounds of interest that are located on grounds accessible to the public. Here is a sampling:

Portsmouth Mound Park is a city park on Hutchins Avenue, just three blocks north of Route 52 in this Scioto County city. Not much remains today but a low, U shaped mound that was once park of a vast earthwork complex that extended across the Ohio River into Kentucky. Nearby were deposits of pipestone used for making pipes, and this has led to speculation that the Great Hopewell Road may have been extended here.

There have been traces of a north/south graded way uncovered at Piketon Mounds in Pike County, along the Scioto between Chillicothe and Portsmouth, that might support this. The Piketon Mounds are on Mound Cemetery Road, one-quarter mile north of Route 32 just east of the junction with Route 23.

In Vinton County an Adena mound is on the shores on man made Lake Hope. While Hope Furnace Mound is not significant, the grounds at Lake Hope State Park are among the prettiest in the state, and an unspoiled reminder of what the area may have looked like to original natives. A network of hiking trails also leads to Hope Furnace, a reminder of early Ohio industrial history that illustrates how iron was manufactured in the 19th century.

The Athens County village of The Plains features the Wolfes Plains Group, a collection of ten Adena mounds. Located just off Route 33 near the city of Athens, The Plains is on a perfectly flat plain near the Hocking River than was an ideal site for mound building.

The first settlers to see the mounds were the original pioneers of Marietta who founded the first town in Ohio in 1788. Showing a rare respect, they tried to preserve the earthworks they found and even established their own cemetery around the largest Adena burial mound, which prevented development and destruction. The Mound Cemetery at 5th and Wooster Streets in Marietta now houses the graves of more Revolutionary War officers than any other cemetery. A few blocks away another mound site has been preserved as Camp Tupper, a public park.

The tallest Adena mound in the state is the Miamisburg Mound in Montgomery County at 65 feet. Today you can climb the 117 steps to the top of the city park overlooking the Miami River. Not far away in Dayton is Sun Watch Village, an excavated Fort Ancient village that has been rebuilt (see page 144).

Indian Mound Reserve, a Greene County Park located on Route 42, just west of Cedarville, offers two examples of ancient earthworks. Trails lead to the Williamson Mound, a 28-foot high Adena burial mound, and to the Pollack Works, a Hopewell embankment. An added bonus here is the spectacular scenery and Cedarcliff Falls on Massies Creek.

The northernmost mounds in Ohio are found in Highbanks Metro Park in southern Delaware County on Route 23 just north of I-270. This site features two Adena mounds as well as an embankment believed to have been built by the Cole people, a later culture that flourished between 1000 and 1300 A.D. These mounds are not spectacular but Highbanks is a Columbus Metro Park and features a visitor's center that has a natural history display that explains mound builder culture at a location accessible to many.

19

Chapter Two:
Forts and Battlefields

After occupying Ohio in relative harmony for thousands of years, the Native Americans completely disappeared from the area within a hundred years of coming into contact with English speaking white men. British fur traders first arrived here in the 1740's and by 1843 the last remaining Ohio-based tribe had left for western reservations. To be sure, they were willing participants in events that accelerated their demise, but they were also caught up in an international struggle with which they were unequipped to cope.

The Europeans' efforts to conquer North America soon spread inland, and Ohio played a unique role. While the native tribes were known to fight each other, the first modern military force to enter what is now Ohio was French. Coming down from Canada, the French had established relations with Ohio Indians as far back as the 1670's, when the explorer LaSalle traveled on Lake Erie and the Ohio River. The French established a trading network and also developed a rapport with the natives. But English traders were also interested in this commerce and intruded with better and cheaper trade goods.

In 1749, the French sent a force of 300 men under Celeron de Bienville to proclaim French sovereignty. Their proclamations were lead plates stating this message placed at major stream confluences. But lead would have to be in a different form to discourage British traders. One Miami chief became known as Old Britain for his partiality and he even invited British traders to build a palisaded post at his village near Piqua (see page 148). In June 1752, this village was attacked by French led renegades who scattered the traders, destroyed the post, and boiled and ate Old Britain.

Full-scale war began two years later when a 22-year-old Virginia militia colonel named George Washington attacked a French party in western Pennsylvania. The French counterattacked and forced Washington to surrender at Fort Necessity, but soon France and England were at war on several continents. As the ultimate goal of the British was colonization rather than commerce, the Indians generally sided with the French, whom they viewed as less of a threat. After several missteps, the British and American numerical strength prevailed and after the fall of Quebec and Montreal, all of French Canada fell into British hands.

The first English speaking military mission into current day Ohio was led by Major Robert Rogers, who traveled along Lake Erie with 200 of his famous Rangers in the fall of 1760. At the mouth of the Cuyahoga River, Rogers was challenged by a chief named Pontiac, who demanded an explanation for his presence. Rogers explained he was en route to Detroit to receive the surrender of the fort there, and proceeded unmolested. The British took over all the French forts on the Great Lakes, but their new monopoly on trade alienated the Indians. By the time the British violated the peace treaty by building a new fort on Sandusky Bay, Indian resentment had peaked.

In spring of 1763, a coalition of eighteen tribes under Pontiac's leadership attacked all of the western forts, with the one on Sandusky Bay being the first to fall. Others were soon destroyed and by summer, the only forts left west of Niagara were Fort Pitt and Detroit. Pontiac himself led the siege of

Detroit for six months, while the siege of Fort Pitt was relieved when British troops under Colonel Henry Bouquet fought their way to the fort. This helped break Pontiac's Conspiracy and in 1764 Bouquet followed up by leading a 1500 man army overland from Fort Pitt to the Tuscarawas River. Here he demanded the return of all captives taken, and his firm actions led to a brief period of peace on the frontier. But the route Bouquet took would be used again fourteen years later in another round of war.

Fort Laurens

Alignments were constantly shifting in the struggle for the Ohio Valley, and by 1776, most Indians felt that the British weren't so bad after all. This was because the specter of American independence was a bigger threat to their land. Most tribes situated between the Americans at Fort Pitt and the British at Detroit sided with the British, although the Delaware in the Tuscarawas Valley remained neutral. In the late fall of 1778, the Americans set out to build a fort in Delaware country to use as a launch for an attack on Detroit.

This force took the same route as Bouquet, but American General Lachlan MacIntosh was no Bouquet. The Americans' supply laden convoy lumbered through the brush, sometimes traveling as little as five miles a day. The Indians noted how disorganized the Americans were and were not awed by MacIntosh's bluster. As it was too late in the year for an active campaign, the Americans built a fort at the present site of Bolivar, and the main force returned to Fort Pitt in December.

Left behind to garrison Fort Laurens were 180 men under Colonel John Gibson. A wise choice, Gibson had the respect of his men and the Delaware, and he also had a good rapport with Moravian missionaries who lived among the Delaware and provided him with information. But the isolated and poorly supplied outpost was seen as an easy target for the British and their Indian allies. In January of 1779, a raiding party ambushed a courier convoy outside the fort and acquired valuable dispatchers. In February a band of British and Indians that included notorious renegade Simon Girty returned to besiege the fort. They announced their presence by surprising a woodcutting detail outside the gates and they killed and scalped all seventeen members within sight of the garrison. The fort was surrounded for the next month and the starving troops were reduced to desperate straits. Many soldiers boiled and ate their own moccasins and two men died from eating poisonous roots. When a hunter managed to bring a deer in, many soldiers eagerly ate it raw.

But the attackers were also hungry, and they eventually abandoned the siege. Yet even the garrison's greatest moment of triumph could not be enjoyed. When a relief convoy laden with supplies approached the fort on March 23, the garrison fired their guns in celebration and stampeded the pack train. Much of the needed supplies were never recovered, and a proposed attack on Detroit was cancelled. Fort Laurens was abandoned in August 1779 and never used again.

Today the site is owned by the Ohio Historical Society. On the 81-acre grounds is a museum that features displays and artifacts unearthed from excavations of the site. There is also a tomb for Ohio's unknown soldier of the Revolution and a picnic grounds that hosts numerous special historical events. For further information about the site at the Bolivar exit of I-77, call 230-874-2059 or 800-283-8914, or write to Ft. Laurens State Memorial, Box 404, 11067, Ft. Laurens Rd., Bolivar, 44696-0404, or go to *www.ohiohistory.org/places/ftlauren.*

Fort Steuben

The victory for Americans in the War of Independence guaranteed freedom for the new country, but created a host of new issues. The new United States had no real source of wealth or income, but western lands were seen as a way to generate income, as they could be sold by the government. But the natives inhabiting these lands had no interest in relinquishing them. And the new country had disbanded its army after winning independence, keeping only eighty soldiers stationed at West Point and Fort Pitt.

24

After the experience of being forced to host British troops, Americans had a distrust of standing armies. Yet it became obvious that troops were needed if the west was to be settled, and Continental Congress authorized the creation of a larger regiment. It also passed the Ordinance of 1785, creating a system of surveying and settling western lands, which became the prototype for all future western expansion.

According to this plan, the west began where the Ohio River crossed the western Pennsylvania border that had just been surveyed, which is at present day East Liverpool. The first section to be surveyed under this plan was a series of seven rows, or ranges, of townships that were six miles square. The first crews of surveyors began work immediately but requested protection from Indians. To protect the surveyors and to evict settlers who were living illegally on land not purchased from the government, the new nation sent troops under Major John Hamtramck in the fall of 1786.

Hamtramck was a native of Belgium who had a noticeable accent, but he understood the situation well enough. Rather than scatter his men to various survey crews, with winter coming on he ordered that a central fort be built for protection in the coming months. The place he selected was a level spot well above the Ohio River that now is a part of downtown Steubenville.

Hamtramck also understood how to motivate his men. With cold weather approaching and only one blockhouse complete, he proposed a contest for the three companies working on the remaining blockhouses. The crew that got done first was to share six gallons of whiskey, the crew finishing second got four gallons, while the last crew to finish would have to dig the footer for the fort stockade. The inspired troops finished all blockhouses in a single weekend.

And none too soon, as a harsh winter came not long afterwards. The garrison of 150 men spent an uneventful winter in a fort that they named for Revolutionary War hero Baron Von Steuben. Fort Steuben was only used for about seven months, as the following spring, most of the garrison was sent downriver to Fort Harmar at the mouth of the Muskingum, where surveying activity was now centered.

But the fort did play a unique role in American history. Not only was it one of the first forts built by the new United States Army, but the survey system it helped inaugurate was used by every other state to enter the union since. Fort Steuben presided over the very beginning of U.S. westward expansion.

The site of Fort Steuben is also unique in how it came to be preserved. In 1986, an organization called Old Fort Steuben bought the site on the 200th anniversary of the fort's construction. The group proceeded to rebuild the fort on its original site entirely with private funds. Also on the grounds today is a gift shop and museum. The fort is open from May to October, while the visitors' center and museum shop are open year round. For more information, contact Historic Fort Steuben, P.O. Box 787, 120 South Third Street, Steubenville, 43952, call 740-283-1787 or go to *www.oldfortsteuben.com*.

Fort Recovery

It is well worth noting that Ohio was the first state to be settled by free U.S. citizens. But settlement could only be accomplished after the new U.S. Army had made the area safe from the many who hoped to help the new nation fail. This included not only the natives who sought to retain their homeland, but European countries as well. In particular were the Spanish, who controlled the Mississippi River and feared U.S. growth, and the British who refused to give up their Great Lakes forts with their lucrative Indian fur trade. Both these nations actively sought Indian alliances to help keep the U.S. from expanding. The British in particular encouraged Indian raids of settlements in the Ohio River Valley. To the Americans it became apparent that isolated forts were insuf-, ficient and some aggressive action must be undertaken. In the fall of 1790, a force of 1,100 men under General Josiah Harmar left Fort Washington in Cincinnati. Harmar's small force of regular professional soldiers was augmented by local militia consisting of citizen soldiers on short-term duty. Marching north, they found only abandoned villages until October 22, when an advance party was lured into an ambush near present-day Fort Wayne, Indiana. The success of the Indians here led to an increase in Indian raids.

The Americans decided the next year to send out a larger army under the leadership of Northwest Territory Governor Arthur St. Clair. Though an experienced soldier, St. Clair was now in his 50s and troubled by gout and ill equipped for the rigors of frontier combat. His army was even less prepared, as the poorly supplied and untrained militia he depended upon were slow to gather at Cincinnati. St. Clair was not able to lead 1,400 men out of Fort Washington until September 1791, but he felt pressured to accomplish something before winter set in.

St. Clair's army was inefficient and slow moving, and stopped for two weeks to construct Fort Hamilton at present day Hamilton. They were also plagued by a lack of supplies and bad weather, which greatly lowered morale. When groups of militia began to desert, St. Clair sent his best regu-

27

lar troops to catch the deserters, which deprived the rest of the army of experienced men. After leaving Fort Jefferson in late October, the army traveled only 29 miles in eleven days before camping along the Wabash River in present day Fort Recovery on the night of November 3.

The next morning they were surprised by an attack from Indian forces from several tribes. While the troops rallied to fight off the attackers, the Indians soon gained the upper hand. The American artillery tried to return fire, but their shots were too high and hit treetops as the Indians trained their fire on officers and artillerymen. St. Clair ordered a retreat that turned into a rout, and his army, now unencumbered by weapons and supplies, made the return trip to Fort Jefferson in a single day. Only the Indian desires for plunder and the killing of captives kept the army from annihilation, but it was still the worst defeat ever suffered by the U.S. Army. Out of 1,400 men, over 900 were killed or captured, and every cannon was left on the field.

St. Clair's Defeat emboldened the Indians and their British allies, and forced the U.S. to address its western problem. St. Clair resigned as commander, although he remained governor, and was replaced by General Anthony Wayne. Taking a studied approach, Wayne recruited and drilled his new force near Pittsburgh for a year and a half. After coming west in 1793, he marched from Cincinnati and began building a series of supply forts. Just before going into winter quarters at Fort Greene Ville, Wayne advanced to the site of St. Clair's Defeat.

On Christmas Eve, Wayne surveyed a field littered with bones, and ordered a fort built on the spot that he decided to call Fort Recovery. The new post was well designed right down to the shutters that covered the musket portholes.

An added bonus was the discovery of the abandoned artillery that the Indians had been unable to haul away. Left under the command of Captain Alexander Gibson, the 200 soldiers of the fort were the troops closest to the front.

That meant they were first in line to be attacked, which is what happened on June 29, 1794. A supply convoy was attacked by a large party of Indians just outside the fort's gates, and after capturing the convoy the Indians impulsively stormed the fort. The well-prepared defenders easily repulsed this attack, although they lost twenty-two men killed and thirty wounded. Getting a taste of defeat discouraged the Indians and many left for home, which left fewer for Wayne to face when he marched north later to do battle.

Today, Fort Recovery State Memorial is an Ohio Historical Society site. There are monuments in downtown Fort Recovery to St. Clair's Defeat and a set of blockhouses, and section of stockade wall has been rebuilt. There is also a museum and research area on the site. For information concerning hours or costs, write to: Fort Recovery State Memorial, Box 532, 1741 Union City Road, Ft. Recovery 45846, or call 419-375-4649 or 800-284-8920, or go to *www.ohiohistory.org/places/ftrecovr.*

Fallen Timbers

Even though it only lasted for about an hour, the Battle of Fallen Timbers was a significant event in American history. Anthony Wayne's well-trained army defeated an Indian coalition that made Ohio safe to settle and began a long period of steady defeat for tribes trying to halt U.S. expansion. In addition to proving that an American army could defeat the Indians on their own, Wayne also practiced a masterful psychological manipulation after the battle that led to Indians ceding Ohio for settlement.

When General Anthony Wayne led 3,000 troops out of Fort Greene Ville in July of 1794, he soon showed how different his army was from St. Clair's. Moving carefully and deliberately, Wayne fortified each campsite against surprise and the Indians soon reported they were facing a foe who did not sleep. Wayne marched to the now abandoned Indian towns at the confluence of the Auglaize and Maumee Rivers and built Fort Defiance in the very heart of Indian country.

Ignoring a plea for more time made by the Indian coalition, Wayne marched down the Maumee and braced for attack. Showing another contrast to St. Clair, he ordered a fort built to deposit all excess baggage so that in case of defeat, these supplies would not be abandoned on the battlefield. In taking a day to do this, he helped foil the Indians, who normally fasted on the day of a battle. This was done for spiritual reasons, but also kept stomach wounds from fatal infection. However, the construction of Fort Deposit made it necessary for the Indians to fast for a second day and fight a battle while hungry.

Wayne continued marching on the north bank of the Maumee on August 20. His army was attacked at a spot where a tornado had felled several large trees that blocked the route. The carefully trained Americans were ready for the attack and after a brief but hard battle they drove the Indians from the field. They continued to pursue their foe towards nearby Fort Miamis, which the British had recently built, in clear violation of a peace treaty. But the British were not willing to risk a war from here, so they denied entrance to the retreating Indians.

Wayne was also reluctant to attack and to create an international incident that might lead to war, which was just what Washington had done 40 years earlier, but Wayne was able to make his point without taking such a risk. After a testy exchange of messages with the British commander, Wayne proceeded to burn all the fields and crops around the fort. Then as a further insult, he rode alone to within firing range and began to survey the fort's defenses. To the Indians watching, this had the effect of showing Wayne's courage and audacity, and proved that he was right when he told them that the British "have neither the power nor the inclination to protect you."

Wayne's psychological operations bore fruit, and the discouraged Tribes sued for peace. The following August, Wayne was able to dictate terms at the Treaty of Greene Ville that guaranteed that Ohio would be safe for settlement. Within a few months of this treaty, American diplomats were able to negotiate England's evacuation of Great Lakes forts like Detroit and the Spanish agreed to open the Mississippi to American shipping. None of this would have been possible without the military victory at Fallen Timbers.

For the Indian tribes, Fallen Timbers marked the beginning of the end. Not only were the Americans now able to deflect them by themselves, but the tribes were no longer able to play off one faction of whites against each other. The

96 years between Fallen Timbers and Wounded Knee were a steady procession of defeats for them.

Though named a national historical park in 2000, the site of the battle is a Toledo Metro Park. The 185-acre site features a monument to Wayne and is located in Lucas County just off the Rt. 24 exit of I-475. The park is free and open year round in daylight hours. For more information write to: Fallen Timbers, Toledo Metro Park Visitors Center, 5100 W. Central Ave., Toledo, 43615 or call 419-535-3050 or 800-860-0149, or go to *www.ohiohistory.org/places/fallen.*

Fort Meigs

The American victory at Fallen Timbers led to seventeen years of relative peace on the frontier, but when conflict resumed the major site of battle was just five miles from the site of Wayne's victory. The War of 1812 was the Indians' last chance to halt American expansion with the help of other nations. A steady flow of settlers since 1795 had led to statehood for Ohio and establishment of new territories. Indians under the leadership of Tecumseh realized that tribal unity was as necessary as outside help if U.S. expansion was to be stopped. The British in Canada who were their trading partners were more than willing to provide that help to gain the use of Indian warriors in a war against the U.S.

The U.S. declared war on Great Britain on June 18, 1812. In the months afterwards, the war effort could not have gone any worse for the Americans. General William Hull, in command of the army in Ohio, left Urbana with 4,000 troops and soon marched north into disaster. To begin with, Hull had been notified of the declaration of war via regular mail, which took several weeks. The British had speedier information, and took advantage by capturing the only American ship on Lake Erie. The American garrison at Fort Michilimackinac in northern Michigan found out they were at war only when informed by the British troops who had already surrounded them. Their surrender led to an order to evacuate Fort Dearborn in Chicago, which was now at risk, and while trying to evacuate this post the garrison was attacked and all were killed or captured.

Hull's army occupied Detroit, but aggressive moves by Tecumseh and the British got them holed up there. The Americans tended to offer high command to aging Revolutionary War vets, but these men had not held field leadership in over thirty years. Paralyzed with fear and indecision, Hull wound up surrendering Detroit and his army without firing a shot on August 16. For this act, he was court martialed and sentenced to death, but his life was spared by President Madison.

With the British now occupying Detroit, American efforts were focused around that city. In January of 1813, another American force successfully raided a supply depot in southern Michigan. But they were surprised by a British counter attack that cost them over 200 men killed and 700 captured. Many of these captives were massacred by Indians, which furthered an American sense of fear and outrage.

The United States gradually came to rely on younger leadership, and new western commander William Henry Harrison was only 38, although he had experience serving as an aid to Wayne. Harrison focused his efforts on the Maumee Rapids near present day Perrysburg. This spot was the head of navigation, so British ships that controlled Lake Erie could proceed no further in their efforts to land behind American lines. Many American forts in the War of 1812 were merely supply depots, but here Harrison sought a permanent fort. To design this, he called upon the services of Colonel Eleazor Wood, a trained engineer and member of the first graduating class of the United States Military Academy at West Point. Wood designed a fortified city capable of hosting 2,000 men in a ten-acre space on a bluff overlooking the Maumee. In addition to a sturdy stockade, Wood also took care to place the fort's gunpowder supply underground, where it could not easily be exploded by enemy shells. Named for Ohio's Governor Return J. Meigs, the new fort was tested in the spring of 1813. Late in April, British war ships carried 1,000 men and sailed up the Maumee, while 1,000 Indian warriors under Tecumseh arrived overland. The British ships on the river had a clear view of the fort's interior, but Wood quickly designed a system of earthworks that shielded the Americans. Despite this lessened visibility, cannon from the Royal Navy ships began a steady bombardment of Fort Meigs, with as many as 500 shells per day fired. The British even fired forge-heated cannon balls in an attempt to blow up the powder magazine that Wood had placed underground. As troops on both sides watched this show, Tecumseh complained that the Americans were holed up "like ground hogs" and refused to fight.

The Americans had limited shells for their artillery to return fire. To correct this situation, Harrison offered an extra whiskey ration for every cannonball turned in that could be sent back to the British. The result of this was that by the end of the siege the Americans had more shells than when they started, but their whiskey supply was considerably depleted.

Harrison could remain calm under fire because he had

gotten word that a large party of Kentucky militia was on its way. He coordinated a plan with them to create a diversion where the militia were to surprise and destroy British artillery along the banks of the Maumee. On May 4, this plan was executed to perfection until the militia followed retreating Indians into the woods and was lured into a deadly ambush. Only 150 out of 800 Kentuckians escaped death or capture, and many captives were massacred until Tecumseh arrived and personally put a stop to the slaughter.

Despite these battle losses, the Americans were still able to withstand the British siege and the warships left on May 9. They returned in July, but were again unable to lure the American ground hogs out into open battle. The only time the site would again play host to a large gathering was in 1840 when 25,000 showed for a rally in support of Harrison's successful presidential campaign.

Today, Fort Meigs State Memorial is a gateway site of the Ohio Historical Society. A six million dollar renovation fixed up the rebuilt fort and added a new museum that opened in 2004. Located off Route 25 just south of Perrysburg, Fort Meigs also hosts several reenactments and special historical events. For more information, contact Fort Meigs State Memorial, Box 3, 29100 W. River Road, Perrysburg, 43552-0003, or call 419-874-4121 or 800-283-8916, or go to *www.ohiohistory.org/places/ftmeigs.*

Fort Stephenson

After failing to capture Fort Meigs in July 1813, a large British and Indian force moved on towards smaller Fort Stephenson. Located in what is today downtown Fremont, Fort

Stephenson was situated at the head of navigation of the Sandusky River beyond which the water was too shallow for ships to sail. With British warships able to shell the fort from the river, it was assumed that the 160 men inside the fort would be overmatched.

In fact, American commanding General William Henry Harrison had ordered the fort evacuated. But he had been talked out of it by Fort Stephenson's ranking officer, 21-year-old Major George Croghan. A nephew of frontier heroes George Rogers Clark and explorer William Clark, Croghan convinced Harrison to delay evacuation, but he soon found himself surrounded and outnumbered by twelve to one.

The fort's defenses had recently been strengthened by Colonel Eleazor Wood, but it remained to be seen if they could withstand a bombardment from the Royal Navy, Croghan himself had only one cannon, a six-pounder nicknamed Old Betsey, whose only previous use had been at the fort's Fourth of July celebration, but Croghan cleverly moved Old Betsey around, firing from different locations, to convince the British he had multiple artillery pieces.

Indian warriors under Tecumseh staged a mock battle to try and lure troops out of Fort Stephenson or from Harrison's main post at Fort Seneca, just eight miles away. But the Americans were not fooled, and with their artillery fire having little effect, the British were forced to try a direct assault. Late in the afternoon of August 2, they began their attack.

Croghan had noticed British fire had concentrated on the fort's northwest corner and he correctly surmised that the assault would strike there. He had Old Betsey wheeled into position and when the British got to the ditch surrounding the fort, they opened fire with any metal they could put down the barrel. This had a devastating effect on the British, who retreated, leaving many casualties. In fact, the British suffered over one hundred killed and wounded, while the Americans had only one man killed and seven wounded.

Soon after, the enemy sailed away in defeat, and the British Navy never again invaded Ohio. Croghan became a national hero, although in a lengthy military career, he never again enjoyed the fame he had at 21.

The site of Fort Stephenson is occupied today by the Birchard Public Library. The library hosts an annual celebration on the anniversary of the attack, and also features exhibits devoted to the battle. The two most famous heroes of the battle have permanent homes on the grounds. Croghan's remains were re-interred on the site in 1906, and Old Betsey is proudly on display on the library lawn. For more information, contact the Birchard Public Library at 423 Croghan Street, Fremont, 43420, or call 419-334-0101 or go to *birchard.lib.oh.us/connect_history.*

Perry's Victory

Though the British were driven from Ohio soil after Fort Stephenson, they still could roam Lake Erie with impunity. The Great Lakes were important in the War of 1812, as the entire region had access to the sea with only a portage around Niagara Falls. Erie and Ontario, the two lakes on either side of this portage, were the ones that both nations sought control over. The United States concentrated efforts on Lake Ontario until in 1813 they finally decided to build a fleet to contest British control of Lake Erie.

In March of 1813, 27-year-old Commodore Oliver Hazard Perry was sent to the shipyards at Presque Isle in

Erie, Pennsylvania. He took over the supervision of construction of a fleet in a harbor protected from British raids by a shallow bar. But this low water also kept his fleet bottled up, since towing his ships over it would leave them helpless in the face of British fire. In August, the British fleet unexpectedly left, and Perry took advantage and launched his fleet.

He sailed towards the American army and met General Harrison on Kelly's Island for an inspection and talks. One thing Perry needed was sailors, as the navy had provided Perry with only the barest of skeleton crews. Between ten and twenty percent of these men were free blacks from New England. Now Perry was aided by volunteers from the Kentucky militia and with this unlikely mix of slaveholders and free blacks, he was able to staff his fleet with about 550 men.

Perry's fleet existed solely to destroy the British fleet, and he was eager for combat. On September 10, 1813, he sailed from Put-In-Bay on South Bass Island with nine ships. However, only two of these carried more than four guns—the *Niagara* and his flagship, the *Lawrence*, each with twenty. The Lawrence was named for Captain James Lawrence, a friend of Perry's who had been killed when his ship battled the British just three months before. Lawrence's dying request of "Don't give up the ship" was emblazoned on a banner that flew on the ship named for him.

Opposing Perry were six British ships of varying size under Commander Robert Barclay. An experienced sailor, Barclay had lost an arm in a British naval victory over Napoleon's fleet at Trafalgar in 1805. Although the opposing fleets had approximately equal number of guns, they were of different types. The British cannons were generally more effective at long range, while the Americans' weapons were better in close quarters. This meant that Perry had to expose his fleet to unanswerable fire as he approached the British. However, the Americans caught a break when a sudden shift put the wind at their back.

The fleet got to within American firing range and began a fierce battle. However, the *Niagara* hung back, out of range, leaving the *Lawrence* to bear the brunt of the British barrage. The decks really did run red with blood as one of the fiercest battles fought in Ohio took place on the open water. Many sailors could not swim, but the decks were even more dangerous, being filled with smoke and fire and wood splintering from cannon balls. The crew of the *Lawrence* fought hard and inflicted great damage on the British, but the gun crews were gradually silenced.

Perry made the decision to strike the colors of the *Lawrence* and move to the *Niagara*. In an open rowboat, he managed to make it to the *Niagara*, where the ship's captain had the nerve to ask how the battle was going. But whatever the motivation for holding the *Niagara* back, it helped contribute to American victory. Storming back into battle with a fresh ship, Perry now had the upper hand. The British had lost many senior officers in the combat, and in trying to maneuver in close quarters under junior officers, the rigging on their two largest ships became entangled. They had to absorb withering fire while drifting, and after a three-and-a-half hour battle, the British surrendered.

Perry's victory message became more famous than Lawrence's last words, as he wrote to Harrison, "We have met the enemy, and they are ours." In addition to gaining a quotable hero, the United States gained the tactical advantage of control of Lake Erie. Now it was the Americans who could land troops behind enemy lines, and the British were forced to abandon Detroit. Harrison's army followed, and in October, defeated the British in the Battle of the Thames, where Tecumseh was killed.

Perry's Victory is commemorated today at Perry's Victory and International Peace Memorial, which also celebrates the world's longest undefended international boundary. Located at Put-In-Bay, the national monument's main feature is a 352 feet high column that was built in 1913 and

41

offers a commanding view of the region. There is also a museum with displays and exhibits. For information on hours and costs, contact Perry's Victory and International Peace Memorial at Box 549, 93 Delaware Avenue, Put-In-Bay, 43456-0549, or call 419-285-2184, or go to *www.nps.gov/pevi/*.

Buffington Island

Exactly fifty years after Perry's Victory, Ohio's sovereign territory was once again invaded, this time from the south. And once again the invasion was repulsed in great part due to the U.S. Navy, this time ending a threat from the Confederacy.

July of 1863 was a significant month for the United States, with major victories at Gettysburg and Vicksburg. But in Ohio, the month brought the war home in the form of Confederate cavalry, as General John Hunt Morgan invaded with 2,500 men. Morgan's raid was supposed to divert attention from troop movements, but the flamboyant General went a step further and crossed the Ohio River on July 8. After terrorizing southern Indiana, Morgan headed on into Ohio.

The chivalrous invaders did sometimes offer to pay for goods with worthless Confederate dollars, but there was also extensive looting and burning. At first, the cavalrymen took frivolous items, but as pursuit of them increased, they were more interested in taking food and fresh horses. And while the citizens of Cincinnati were in a panic about being attacked, Morgan's men preferred the less crowded back roads of southern Ohio. After wreaking havoc briefly, Morgan's main concern was re-crossing the Ohio at a shallow spot.

His scouts had told him of an excellent spot at Buffington Island in Meigs County where the river was normally only two feet deep in summer. Since Ohio had last been invaded, the invention of steamboats, trains, and the telegraph had made the transfer of people and information much faster. While the Union used these inventions to try and catch the rebels, Morgan also had his own telegrapher eavesdrop and spread false information over the lines. But being constantly on the run began to wear down the invaders, who no longer had time to get off the saddle for much needed sleep.

Among the thousands of Union soldiers trying to catch Morgan was the 23rd Ohio Regiment, which featured two Ohio natives who defended their state and would go on to the Presidency. The regimental commander was Colonel Rutherford Hayes and one of his officers was William McKinley, who enlisted as a private but rose to major. Their regiment got close enough to fire at Morgan's men, although on the day of battle they had been shipped across the Ohio to capture Confederates who made it across the river.

Morgan approached Buffington Island on July 18, but he lost valuable time trying to find a guide and did not make it to the ford until after dark. He hoped to make a successful crossing in the morning with his remaining 1,900 men. But at sunrise on July 19, he was caught by cavalry under General Henry Judah following along the river, and cavalry under General Edward Hobson coming overland. Not only was he outnumbered four to one, but even the weather turned against him. Recent rain had swelled the Ohio to a depth of six feet, which was not only too deep for fording but was deep enough that navy gunboats could safely pass.

A flotilla under Commander Leroy Fitch of the U.S.

43

Navy had sailed up to block Morgan's escape. Fitch's flagship was the *Moose*, a sternwheeler that had been plated with tin and supplied with four cannons. As the fog lifted, the *Moose* began firing at the Confederates on the Ohio shore. Trapped on three sides, Morgan's only hope was to hold off the enemy long enough to escape upstream along the Ohio. Morgan and about 1,100 men were able to do this, but over 700 men were captured at Buffington Island.

Morgan found another shallow spot near Reedsville, a few miles upstream, and tried to cross there. About 360 of his men did make it across the Ohio before Fitch's ships showed up and began firing at them. Morgan himself was actually mid-river at this point, and could have safely escaped, but he chose to remain with the bulk of his command. He now began a desperate ride across Ohio against increasing odds that ended with his surrender in Columbiana County on July 26.

Morgan was treated as a thief rather than as a prisoner of war, and he and his officers were sent to the Ohio Penitentiary and treated harshly. However, Morgan and six others dug a tunnel and escaped in November of 1863. He was killed not long after returning to Confederate lines, and since his time Ohio has remained safe from the ravages of the French army, the British navy, and the Confederate cavalry. Buffington Island has been listed as a threatened Civil War site as a gravel mining operation is working over much of the site. Left undisturbed is a four-acre park with a monument and restrooms. Just down the road along State Route 124 is a monument to Major Daniel McCook. One of three union officers killed in the battle, the 63-year-old McCook is better known as the father of the Fighting McCooks family of generals. (See page 84). For more information on Buffington Island, call 888-909-6446, or visit their website at *www.ohiohistory.org/places/buffingt/.*

Chapter Three:
The Underground Railroad

The two biggest challenges facing the Constitutional framers were westward expansion and slavery, and Ohio was at the forefront of both. In the Ordinance on 1787, the Continental Congress prohibited slavery in the newly established Northwest Territory. This was the first step in a westward expansion policy that included a divide between those states and southern states, where slavery would be permitted. It was the result of considerable Congressional haggling to seek a balance between free and slave states.

The original northern states gradually came to prohibit slavery, but the plantation economy of the south had already become dependent on slave labor. While more progressive southern leaders acknowledged that slavery would eventually have to be abolished, the drafters of the U.S. Constitution were unable to satisfactorily address the issue. In a compromise that only postponed dealing with the problem, slaves were counted for population purposes as three-fifths of a person while importation of additional slaves was prohibited after a certain date.

The failure of the Constitutional framers to fully address slavery gave legal legitimacy to the concept of slaves as property. There was nothing even to prevent a slaveholder from impregnating his slave to increase his property and even sell his offspring for a profit. With no more rights than equipment or livestock, slaves running away were essentially stealing themselves from their masters. But when caught,

46

slaves were returned to their masters for punishment rather than jailed since an imprisoned slave was of no use to its owner.

However, those who assisted runaway slaves in escaping could be subjected to imprisonment. In 1793, Congress passed the Fugitive Slave Law, which mandated the return of escaped slaves and stipulated penalties for those who helped them. As opposition to slavery grew, and the issue grew to be the most contentious and emotional issue facing the nation, many chose to flout this law. An unofficial and illegal network evolved that came to be known as the Underground Railroad.

The "railroad" part of the name wasn't added until 1835 or so when railroads were becoming more common, but the network flourished and grew between 1820 and 1860. Traffic increased after a more restrictive fugitive slave law was passed in 1850. Ohio was right in the middle of this controversial enterprise. On the eastern border of Ohio, it was only about one hundred miles from the Ohio River, below which slavery was legal, to Lake Erie, above which lay Canada and freedom. This narrow hinge made Ohio a swing state of a different sort and led to the state becoming a hot- bed of abolitionism, and an active home of the Underground Railroad.

Ohio's 425-mile border of the Ohio River had 23 known locations where slaves crossed to freedom, and at least ten Lake Erie ports in the state shipped escapees to Canada. Since this activity was illegal, no official records were kept, but it is believed that as many as 80,000 slaves could have passed through Ohio on the Underground Railroad. While many citizens were involved and sympathetic, many were also opposed, and the law favored this group.

According to state law, any free blacks living in Ohio not only had to produce papers proving that they were free, but were also required to post a cash bond to show they would not be a financial drain on the community. Bounty hunters from slave states frequently came to Ohio to retrieve escaping property, and many were not above kidnapping free blacks as replacements. The courts were not only obligated to impose criminal punishments for those aiding the escapees, but there are also records of civil cases where abolitionists were ordered to compensate slaveholders for successful assistance to runaways. Abolitionists were also frequent targets of harassment or mob violence from pro-slavery forces.

The people who risked so much to aid escaping slaves were often religiously motivated, with Quakers, Presbyterians, and Methodists being particularly active. Many free blacks and escaped slaves also risked their freedom to aid their brethren. All of their efforts were shrouded in secrecy, but in 1890, an Ohio State University history professor named Wilbur Siebert collected information on the Underground Railroad from surviving participants that presented a clearer picture.

Though it used similar terminology, the Underground Railroad was not a railroad but an interlocking network. Escaping slaves who made it across the Ohio River were sheltered at "stations" where they were temporarily hidden. Then, traveling under cover of darkness, they were taken by "conductors" to the next station along the line to be hidden again. There were many interlocking lines of the "railroad" and passengers were often shunted sideways to throw off pursuers. Eventually, the escapees would get to Lake Erie, where passage to Canada could be arranged with sympathetic ship operators.

48

Stationmasters often constructed networks of hideaways and tunnels to shelter passengers, and conductors used wagons with hidden compartments to transport them. Conductors only dealt with people they were sure they could trust, and many were later able to boast that they never lost a single passenger to slave hunters. Many courageous former slaves returned to slave states frequently to retrieve more escapees despite the risks involved for them.

Underground Railroad routes crossed all over Ohio with Siebert estimating they covered up to 3,000 miles of routes with over 400 stations. Some places stood out as centers of abolitionist activity and still have memorials accessible to attest to their standing. Here are a few of the more outstanding examples.

Cincinnati

The Ohio River served as a nearly 1,000-mile border between free and slave states. As the largest city on that border, Cincinnati was at the center of much conflict over slavery. The city was a major steamboat port that hosted southern travelers and their slaves. And when the river froze over in winter, runaways crossed over here seeking the anonymity of the city. By 1829, Cincinnati was home to 2,258 free black citizens, but anti-black riots that year reduced the total to 740 within five years.

Despite the racial hostility and mobs that threatened anti-slavery activists, there was a strong tradition of abolitionism in the city. The patrician Nicholas Longworth was just one of the many civic leaders who opposed slavery. Activity in the city was not limited to helping slaves escape on

49

the Underground Railroad. The city also throbbed with print- ers and scholars denouncing slavery and the many court cases involving slave related issues often attracted lawyers who worked for free. Among the Cincinnati attorneys who did pro bono work on behalf of slaves were Salmon P. Chase and Rutherford B. Hayes.

In 1832, the Reverend Lyman Beecher came to town as President of the newly established Lane Theological Semi- nary. He brought his New England abolitionist sentiments - and his 21-year-old daughter Harriet- with him. She married a Lane professor named Calvin Stowe in 1836, and their house became an active station on the Underground Railroad, while she compiled research on a novel that would rock the nation (see page 116).

The most active Underground Railroad member in Cin- cinnati was Levi Coffin. Known unofficially as the President of the Underground Railroad, Coffin claimed to have helped over 3,000 slaves escape. A Quaker who was born in North Carolina in 1798, Coffin's attempts to educate slaves were met by threats. Like many southern born Quakers, he moved to the north where he could put his beliefs into practice. From Newport, Indiana, Coffin became an active conductor on the Underground Railroad.

In 1847, he moved to Cincinnati, where he became even more active. As a merchant, he opened a free labor store that only sold goods produced by non-slave labor. Located at 6th and Elm Streets, Coffin's large store also served as shelter for runaways, and he constructed a network of tunnels to hide and transport his passengers.

The best place to learn about the efforts of Coffin and others is the newly built National Underground Railroad Freedom Center. Located along Cincinnati's waterfront, this 158,000 square foot facility is a good starting point. Exhibits include an actual slave pen, interactive exhibits simulating escape from slavery, and films and displays that lead to discussion on many freedom related issues. The center is open year round except for Mondays and Thanksgiving and Christmas. For more information on hours, costs and tours, contact: National Underground Railroad Freedom Center, 50 E. Freedom Way, Cincinnati, 45202, or call 513-333-7500 or toll free 877-648-4838 or go online at *www.freedomcenter.org.*

Ripley

While Cincinnati hosted considerable activity on the Underground Railroad, the bulk of the work was carried out in many small towns throughout the state. One of the foremost river towns involved was Ripley in Brown County, where thousands crossed the Ohio to freedom. Once across, many sought refuge at the Liberty Hill home of John Rankin, where a beacon in a front window was visible from the Ohio.

Rankin, a Presbyterian minister, was born in the south, where he was revolted by the practice of slavery. He moved north to Ripley in 1821, and a few years later, published a book called *Letters on American Slavery*, a series of letters to his brother in the south that detailed his objections to the institution. In 1828, Rankin was named President of Ripley College, and he moved to a hilltop home overlooking a broad expanse of the Ohio. For the next 35 years, he and his wife Jane and their nine sons and four daughters maintained an active Underground Railroad station from the home, aiding over 2,000 fugitives. Runaways could climb 100 steps up Liberty Hill towards Rankin's beacon light and be assured of safe shelter and passage to the next station accompanied by one of Rankin's sons.

Rankin was very publicly opposed to slavery, and even founded the Ohio Anti-Slavery Society in Zanesville in 1834. But he was never caught breaking the fugitive slave law and none of the slaves he helped escape was ever captured. It was in the course of discussion with other abolitionists that Rankin revealed the story of Eliza, a slave girl he had helped. Carrying her baby and pursued by hounds, Eliza had crossed the Ohio in winter when it was nearly frozen over, but she had to contend with standing water between ice floes, and Rankin told the story to Harriet Beecher Stowe, who depicted it in a dramatic scene in her famous novel *Uncle Tom's Cabin.*

The Ohio Historical Society purchased the Rankin House in 1938, and today it is a museum filled with Rankin memorabilia. For more information on hours and fees, contact the Rankin House, 6152 Rankin Hill Road, Ripley, 45167, or call 937-392-1627 or toll free 800-752-2705. Or go to *www.ohiohistory.org/places/rankin/.*

Many of the conductors helping runaway slaves cross the Ohio River were former slaves themselves. Among them were Mr. And Mrs. Orrin Gould, who operated a livery in Wheelersburg, and James Dicher of Ironton, who was known as "the red fox of the underground." But John Parker of Ripley was the most impressive of these in many ways.

An experienced foundry man, Parker had the physical strength expected of a blacksmith. But he was also intelligent enough to acquire several patents and write his autobiography, and a successful businessman who had many employees. Yet he regularly risked everything to cross into Kentucky to aid slaves seeking freedom. Parker was so hated by Kentucky slavers that a reward was posted for his capture dead or alive, which meant essentially the best he could hope for if caught was a quick death. Consequently, he never went out without his pistols and knife.

John P. Parker was born in Virginia in 1827, the son of a white man and a slave woman. This meant he was born a slave, and at the age of eight, he was sold and forced to walk in chains from Richmond to Mobile, Alabama. But Parker showed an aptitude for mechanical and foundry work, and a benevolent owner let him keep the wages he earned. While still a young man, Parker saved enough to purchase himself from his master. He immediately moved north of the Ohio, married a Cincinnati girl, and located in Ripley in 1849.

Here he operated a prosperous forge by day and rowed across the Ohio to help slaves escape by night. He is said to have led 900 slaves to freedom, and he escaped from many tight spots himself that he recounted in his autobiography. After the Civil War he became involved in manufacturing farm machinery and also expanded into the milling business.

All of his six children entered professions and several of them graduated from college.

In 1996, the John P. Parker Historical Society purchased Parker's former riverfront home for a museum that is now open to the public. For more information, contact John P. Parker House, 300 Front Street, Ripley, 45167, or call 937-392-4188 or go to *www.johnparkerhouse.org*.

Westerville

The abundance of abolitionist literature was not the only example of artistic influence on the political landscape. In at least one case, a popular song written in Ohio made a significant contribution to the anti-slavery movement.

In 1842, an escaped slave named Joseph Selby arrived in the Pickaway County village of Rushville in poor shape. He was looking for William Hanby, a local saddle and harness maker. Hanby had earlier served as an indentured servant to pay off debts, and his experience hardened his attitude towards involuntary servitude to where he became active in the active underground. But he was also a circuit-riding minister who was on the road a lot, and in his absence Joseph Selby wound up being sent to Dr. Simon Hyde, another Underground Railroad conductor.

Dr. Hyde had determined that Selby had contracted pneumonia crossing the Ohio in winter, and the illness proved fatal. But before he died, Selby told Hanby of his plans to return to the south to retrieve his lost love named Nellie Gray. He mourned that his darling had been taken from him and sold down the river to the deep south, where escape was unlikely. Hanby related this sad tale to his young son Benjamin, who later began working on a song about the ill-fated lovers.

In 1854, the Hanbys moved to Westerville. Their neighbor was Reverend Lewis Davis, the President of Otterbein College and an active participant in the Underground Railroad. Hanby continued his work aiding escapees, and he and Davis used their barns to shelter refugees, who were transported onward by Benjamin Hanby, who was now a student at Otterbein. In 1856, Benjamin Hanby completed his ballad, which he copyrighted under the title, "My Darling Nellie Gray." The song quickly became a national hit, and reinforced notions about the cruelty of slavery. Despite its contemporary significance, the song is seldom heard today, though this is not true of all Hanby tunes. While living in the Westerville house, Hanby also composed the popular Christmas song, "Up On the House Top."

Today this house in an Ohio Historical Site open to the public. For more information, contact Hanby House State

Memorial, Box 1063, 160 W. Main Street, Westerville, 43068 or call 614-891-6289, or toll free 800-600-6843, or go to *www.ohiohistory.org/places/hanby.*

Mt. Pleasant

In many cases, entire communities became known as havens for fugitive slaves. Some examples of this were Salem in Columbiana County, Marengo in Morrow County, Xenia in Greene County and Springboro in Warren County. Many of these towns owed their activities to Quaker roots. A prime example of this was the Jefferson County village of Mount Pleasant, where five former Underground Railroad stations are still standing. The town was established by Quakers, who built a meeting house in 1814 that is now the Quaker Yearly Meeting House State Memorial. The Quakers were known for their abolitionist views, and Mt. Pleasant's citizens were particularly strident on the matter.

It was here in 1817 that Charles Osborne founded the newspaper *The Philanthropist*, the first publication to advocate abolishing slavery. One of his contributors was Benjamin Lundy, who founded Ohio's first anti-slavery organization in St. Clairsville. In 1821, Lundy moved to Mt. Pleasant and launched an abolitionist monthly magazine called *The Genius of Universal Emancipation.* To get his material to the printer, Lundy walked to Steubenville and stayed overnight at the home of Benjamin Stanton, an uncle of Edwin Stanton. The printer who published the work was James Wilson, grandfather of Woodrow Wilson. The peripatetic Lundy soon moved on, and in his long career he claimed to have traveled over 25,000 miles crusading against slavery.

The Quakers of Mt. Pleasant were industrious and without expensive vices, and the town prospered. Several community members built fine brick homes. And in the homes of Jonathan Binns, John Hogg, George Jenkins, David Updegraff and Lundy, there were also trap doors and secret passageways to shelter their Underground Railroad passengers. In addition to hosting state anti-slavery conventions, the residents also started a Free Labor Store, where they boycotted slavery by selling only goods made from free labor.

The picturesque hilltop village retains its heritage today. The town of 500 has six museums and in 1974 the entire community was designated a National Historic Landmark. In 2000, Mt. Pleasant was designated as a National Historic Landmark District of the Underground Railroad. The Historic Society of Mt. Pleasant owns many of the sites in town, but some Underground Railroad stops are still private homes. Most sites are open by appointment only, although you can stroll the village anytime. Tours can be arranged by calling 800-752-2631 or online at *users.1stnet/gudzent/*.

Oberlin

Northeast Ohio was fertile ground for the abolitionist movement. This area of the state, known as the Western Reserve, was settled by New Englanders who were generally opposed to slavery. John Brown, the most fiery abolitionist of all, was raised in Hudson and later lived in Kent, Richfield and Akron. Akron was also where famed Underground Railroad conductor Sojourner Truth made her famous "Ain't I A Woman" speech. But the town most noted for anti-slavery activity was Oberlin, which one author has called "the town that started the Civil War."

Central to this activity was Oberlin College, the first interracial and co-educational college in the country. The college was founded by abolitionists and always pursued a strong course against slavery. The most famous incident involving the town occurred in 1858 when a mob stormed a building in nearby Wellington where a recaptured fugitive slave was incarcerated. The scene of an angry mob eager to get their hands on a black prisoner was sadly all too common in American history, but this case was different. This time the mob's purpose was to free rather than lynch the prisoner, and they succeeded.

Among the 37 raiders from Oberlin were free blacks such as brothers Wilson and Henry Evans, who were Underground Railroad conductors, and John Mercer Langston, an Oberlin College graduate who was the first black lawyer and elected public official in Ohio and who later became a Congressman, minister to Haiti, and the dean of Howard University. The Wellington rescue proved immensely controversial

59

and resulted in a lengthy trial in Cleveland. The defendants spent months in jail, but ultimately only two were convicted of reduced charges.

The next year the even more controversial John Brown, whose father had been an Oberlin College trustee, made his famous raid on Harper's Ferry in an ill-fated attempt to start a slave uprising. Among those who were executed along with Brown were three black men from Oberlin, including the grandfather of author Langston Hughes. Sympathetic Oberlin neighbors retrieved their bodies for interment in the town's Westwood Cemetery.

The area's literary connection to civil rights continues today, as Lorain County native Toni Morrison used the true tale of an escaped slave who killed her daughter rather than let her be returned to slavery as the focal point of her Pulitzer Prize winning novel *Beloved*. Oberlin also preserves its progressive reputation today, and the private home of conductor Wilson Evans is a National Historic Landmark. The Oberlin Heritage Center/Oberlin Historical Improvement Organization offers a tour of area sites that includes the former home of Oberlin professor and abolitionist Congressman James Monroe. For information, call 440-774-1700 or write to the Oberlin Heritage Center at 73 1/2 South Professor Street, Box 455, Oberlin, 44074 or go to *www.oberlinheritage.org*. The Lorain County Visitor's Bureau also offers a self-guided driving tour of 15 Underground Railroad sites that includes Westwood Cemetery and monuments to the Wellington Rescue and John Brown. To find out more, call 800-334-1673 or go to *www.loraincountychamber.com/*.

Ashtabula

The goal of fugitive slaves in Ohio was to make it to Lake Erie, where they might obtain passage to Canada, where slavery had been abolished in 1793 and the Fugitive Slave Laws did not apply. Ohio ports where sympathetic steamer captains ferried fugitives included Toledo, Sandusky, Huron, Vermilion, Lorain, Cleveland, Fairport Harbor and Ashtabula. A particularly sympathetic haven was the Ashtabula area, where locals boasted that no slave was ever captured within the borders of Ashtabula County.

Among the leading abolitionists was prominent local merchant William Hubbard. He and his wife Catherine built a mansion at Walnut Street and Lake Avenue that became the terminus of several lines of the Underground Railroad. Overlooking Lake Erie, this active stop became known as Mother Hubbard's Cupboard and the Grand Emporium. Hubbard hid fugitives in his cellar or hayloft in his barn and even built a tunnel that led to the lake. Today this home has been restored as the William Hubbard House and Underground Railroad Museum. For more information, write to them at Box 266, Ashtabula, 44005 or call 440-964-8168 or go to *hubbardhouseugrrmuseum.org*.

In the nearby county seat of Jefferson, the law office of former Congressman Joshua Giddings has been restored and is open by appointment. A fiery abolitionist, Giddings was forced to resign his seat for denouncing slavery, in violation of Congressional rules, but he was immediately returned to office by his constituents. Giddings also hid runaways in a spare room of his law office. To arrange a tour of this building at 108 North Chestnut Street, call 440-466-7337 or go to *ashtcohs.com*.

Also in the area is Unionville's Old Tavern, which is just on the Lake County side of the Ashtabula-Lake County line. Built in 1818, the tavern was an active Underground Railroad stop that took advantage of its location near the lake and along the Cleveland to Buffalo stagecoach route. Harriet Beecher Stowe was a guest, and while here heard the tale of the rescue of a fugitive slave that she incorporated into her novel *Uncle Tom's Cabin*. The tavern is still open as a restaurant today. For more information, call 800-782-8376.

Other sites

There are several other Underground Railroad sites in Ohio that are open to the public. Here are some of them.

The Samuel Moore house in Circleville today houses the genealogy library of the Pickaway County Historical Society. A plaque in front of the building explains the site's significance as a station. This is a part of a series of ten historical markers installed in 2004 by ODOT and the Friends of Freedom Society to note the River-to-Lake Freedom Trail between Portsmouth and Sandusky.

The Kelton House at 586 East Town Street in Columbus (43215) has been restored and is a museum operated by the Junior League. Built in 1852 by Fernando and Sophie Kelton, this home was an active station where escapees were hidden in the barn or cistern or surrounding wooded area. One ten-year-old runaway girl wound up living with the family and was even married in the home. To find out more, call 614-469-2022 or go to *keltonhouse.com.*

The Belmont County community of Flushing was an active Underground Railroad location because of Quakers living there. Today, John Mattox, a descendent of slaves, has opened an Underground Railroad museum at 121 High Street. To get more information or arrange a tour, write to Box 47, Flushing, 43977, call 740-968-2080, or go to *ugrrf.org*.

In the Muskingum County village of Trinway, the home of George Willison Adams now houses the G.W. Adams Educational Center and a Bed and Breakfast. Built in 1856, the 29-room mansion is on the National Register of Historic Places. Adams was a Virginia native who came to Ohio in 1808. He got involved in the milling business in nearby Dresden, but also became so involved in sheltering runaways that he built a tunnel between his home and the Muskingum River. To find out more, call 740-754-2336 or go to *prospectplace-dresden.com*.

In Stark County, the J. Ridgeway Haines house in Alliance has been purchased by the Alliance Area Preservation Society in hopes of being made into a museum. Haines, a Quaker who was active in anti-slavery organizations, hid fugitives in an upstairs room, and the house is now on the National Register of Historic Places. For more information, call 330-829-4668 or go to *haineshouse.org*.

Also in Stark County is Spring Hill in Massillon, another home that is on the National Register of Historic Places. Built in the 1820s by Quakers, the home was later purchased by Arvine Wales, who continued the previous owners' work as station keepers on the Underground Railroad. The home features a secret stairway to a closet that was used to shelter runaways. The site is now maintained by the Massillon Museum Foundation. To find out more, write to 1401 Springhill Lane NE, Massillon, 44646-2500 or call 330-833-6749 or go to *www.massillonproud.com/springhill/*.

Chapter Four:
Civil War Generals

After 1850 it became increasingly obvious that only war could bridge the widening chasm between slave and free states. Abraham Lincoln's election to the Presidency in 1860 was the final straw that led to secession of several southern states. In the convulsive Civil War that followed, Ohio provided over 300,000 troops to the Union Army, which ranked third among states.

With the rival capitals of Washington and Richmond only 100 miles apart, much of the war effort focused on that sector. Here the Union forces foundered badly the war's early years despite the North's superiority in soldiers and supplies. Lincoln changed commanders six times in two years in an unsuccessful attempt to defeat Robert E. Lee's Army of Northern Virginia.

West of the Appalachian Mountains, the federal army experienced greater success. Many Ohio troops were sent to this front, and some native Ohioans who led them gradually found positions of prominence. Some of these generals, like Rutherford Hayes, James Garfield and Benjamin Harrison did not attain fame in war but later went on to become president (see Chapter Five). Others, such as Alexander McCook of Carrollton and James McPherson of Clyde, whose home at Maple Street and McPherson Highway is open for tours, became competent corps commanders who played key roles in major battles. Some, such as Don Carlos Buell of Washington County and William Rosecrans of Delaware County were in command of Union forces in major battle in western campaigns. But it was three men raised in Ohio whose success was essential to eventual Union victory. Philip Sheridan of Somerset parlayed his success in the west into independent command in the east where his devastation of Virginia's Shenandoah Valley cut off valuable supplies to the Confederacy. William Sherman of Lancaster rose to become overall commander in the west and his capture of Atlanta and subsequent destructive March to the Sea helped re-elect Lincoln and hasten the end of the war. Ulysses Grant of Georgetown offered the best example of Ohio-bred leadership. After victory and Forts Henry and Donelson, Shiloh, Vicksburg and Chattanooga, Grant was chosen by Lincoln as overall Union commander. By a series of ruthless and relentless attacks in which thousands died, Grant was able to succeed where others had failed.

What all three men had in common besides an Ohio upbringing was the realization that the goal of the warrior is to end war as quickly as possible, and in total war this involves harsh measures concerning destruction of enemy resources and sacrificing your own men. Sheridan and Sherman were both reviled for mass destruction but their methods ultimately saved lives by shortening the war. Grant's attacks resulted in terrible Union casualties but he knew he could replace his losses while the Confederacy was running out of manpower.

In addition to these prominent leaders, Ohio also produced some of the more interesting generals of the conflict. George Custer of New Rumley became a general at the age of 23, and this hard driving, ambitious and flamboyant cavalry commander later went on to Indian warfare and died in the most famous defeat in U.S. history. The McCook family of Carrollton was unique in that two brothers produced a combined total of six sons who attained the rank of general.

Sites pertaining to these leaders are accessible and for once a historic tour of Ohio can be arranged geographically as locations for these generals are all on a line that follows U.S. Routes 68 and 22 and State Route 9.

Ulysses S. Grant

When the Civil War began, the man ultimately credited with saving the Union was a lowly store clerk in Galena, Illinois. But Ulysses S. Grant had come from humble roots, so it is not surprising that he was still unknown while waiting for opportunity. Grant was born in 1822 in the Ohio River village of Point Pleasant (see page 88). His father, Jesse Grant, was a farmer and tanner who the next year moved his family to the Brown County town of Georgetown.

Grant grew up in this sleepy county seat in modest circumstances. He disliked tannery work but enjoyed farming, particularly when he could work with horses. In addition to being a superior horseman, Grant was also a good student and in 1839, he received an appointment to the United States Military Academy at West Point. He graduated in 1843 and entered the army as a lieutenant.

After peace time service in Missouri and Louisiana Grant saw action when the Mexican War began in 1846. Under the command of Zachary Taylor, Grant served with distinction and was promoted to captain. When the war was over, Grant married Julia Dent, but she did not accompany her husband to some of the isolated frontier outposts he was assigned to. By 1854, Grant was bored by peacetime military service and hated living without his family in Humboldt, California. He began drinking heavily and neglecting his duties and wound up resigning his commission rather than risk court martial. He returned east on funds borrowed from Simon Bolivar Buckner, a fellow officer and former West Point classmate. He then moved to Missouri where he tried farming and real estate, but failed in both. By 1861, he was reduced to clerking in his family's leather goods store.

When the Civil War began, Grant's military background got him a commission as a colonel in an Illinois regiment. He was sent to Cairo, Illinois, where the Ohio and Mississippi Rivers meet. In the Civil War, the North tended to name their armies and battles after rivers, while the South employed the names of states or towns. This may have been an indication that the Union saw the inland waterways as a crucial front, especially in the west, where Midwestern crops used the Mississippi for transport. The Union also hoped to split the South by gaining control of the Mississippi.

In February 1862, Grant advanced on Fort Henry on the Tennessee River. He captured this fort easily and moved on to nearby Fort Donelson, which was held by a larger force under Grant's old friend Buckner. After a Confederate counterattack failed, Grant was able to bottle up the Confederates, and Buckner asked for surrender terms. Grant gave his friend no special consideration, replying that "no terms except unconditional and immediate surrender can be accepted." Buckner apparently held no grudge towards Grant, as years later when Grant faced financial reverses (see page 118), Buckner again offered funds and he also served as a pall bearer at Grant's funeral.

Acceptance of these terms gave Grant hero status and a new nickname that his initials stood for "Unconditional Surrender." This was ironic, since Grant was born Hiram Ulysses Grant, but had changed his name before going to West Point to avoid the initials H.U.G.

Grant then moved up the Tennessee River, where his army was attacked at Shiloh on April 6. Although he was caught by surprise, Grant rallied his men and held off the attack in a bloody, two-day battle. But when a higher-ranking officer arrived afterwards, Grant was relegated to a meaningless second-in-command role. He considered resigning, but was talked out of it by Sherman and was then shortly restored to overall command.

Other Union successes on western rivers had left Vicksburg as the only major point on the Mississippi still controlled by the Confederates. Grant was assigned the task of capturing the city, and spent several months unsuccessfully trying various engineering schemes to bypass the rebel army. Finally in the spring of 1863, he was able to isolate his foe, and he used aggressive action to fend off any attempts at reinforcement. After a prolonged siege, Vicksburg surrendered on July 4, 1863 and the Confederacy was split in two. His status rapidly rising, Grant was next sent to Chattanooga, where Union forces were bottled up. Working with fellow Ohioans Sherman, Sheridan and MacPherson, he fought his way out with victories at Lookout Mountain and Missionary Ridge.

Lincoln now promoted Grant to Lieutenant General and brought him east as overall Union commander. The Union Army in the east had already gone through several commanders and found all of them wanting. The first was Irwin McDowell, a native of Columbus who was pressured into doing battle before he or his army was ready. George McClellan served two stints in charge, but he was so overly cautious about using his superior numbers that Lincoln allegedly asked if it was all right to borrow the army for a while since McClellan wasn't using it. John Pope was most known for boasting that his headquarters was in the saddle, which caused Confederates to quip that his headquarters was where his hindquarters should be. Ambrose Burnside was best known for his side-whiskers which gave us the name sideburns, while Joseph Hooker lent his name to the prostitutes who followed the army. George Meade, appointed right before Gettysburg, was a competent general but got along with no one, and Grant was brought in over him.

It is said that when Lincoln was told of Grant's drinking, he suggested the same brand be distributed to the other generals. There is no confirmation to this story, but Lincoln clearly expressed his pleasure with Grant in saying, "I can't spare this man—he fights." In a five-week period in spring of 1864, Grant hammered at Lee relentlessly in an attempt to get to Richmond. This series of attacks cost the Union Army over 50,000 in dead and wounded, which alarmed and shocked many. When questioned about these attacks, Grant replied, "I propose to fight it out on this line if it takes all summer."

What distinguished this from mere stubbornness was the awareness that the Union losses could be replaced, but those inflicted on Lee's army were more permanent. Unlike his predecessors, Grant used his larger numbers to his advantage, and by summer he was entrenched at Petersburg just a few miles from Richmond. Here they were bogged down in siege warfare, but victories elsewhere by Sherman and Sheridan helped hasten the collapse of the Confederacy.

In the spring of 1865, southern defenses fell, and Richmond was taken. Lee tried to escape but Grant's army pursued them to Appomattox Court House, where Lee surrendered on April 9. It was the third time in 38 months that Grant had compelled a large Confederate army to lay down their weapons. It is worth noting that the first man to surrender to him (Buckner) had a son who became a general in World War II, while the last man to surrender to him (Lee) was a son of a general who was in the American Revolution.

By now Grant could offer more gracious terms that belied his "Unconditional Surrender" moniker. In keeping with Lincoln's hopes to bind the nation's wounds, Grant generously allowed the defeated soldiers to keep some arms and equipment, which also served to encourage other armies still in the field to consider surrender. It is not surprising that Grant was the next person elected President after Lincoln.

The home where Grant lived from his first year until he left for West Point is open today at 219 East Grant Avenue and operated by the Ohio Historical Society. This is largely due to the efforts of John Ruthven, an Ohio Valley wildlife painter in the tradition of John James Audubon. A native of Cincinnati, who now has a studio in Georgetown, Ruthven and his wife Judy purchased the Grant home and donated it to the state. For further information, write to the Grant Homestead Association, 318 West State Street, Georgetown, 45121, or call (937) 378-4222 or go to *www.ohiohistory.org/places/grantboy/index.*

William Tecumseh Sherman

Grant had considerable help in winning the Civil War, and foremost among his helpers was fellow Buckeye William Tecumseh Sherman. Born in Lancaster in 1820, Sherman was the sixth of eleven children born to Judge Charles Sherman, a lawyer and Justice of the Ohio Supreme Court. But his father's death in 1829 resulted in the children being scattered among different homes to be raised. William wound up in the home of Thomas Ewing, a political ally of his father's and a U.S. Senator. While he grew up in the Ewing household, he was never formally adopted, which made things simpler when he later married Ewing's daughter.

His connections no doubt helped tall, redheaded Sherman secure an appointment to West Point, but he showed his abilities by graduating sixth in the class of 1840. After graduation, he served in the South until he was sent to California during the Mexican War. He served credibly here and in 1850 married Ellen Ewing in Washington, D.C. where her father was serving as Secretary of the Interior. In 1853 Sherman resigned from the army and returned to California to enter the banking business. He did well in San Francisco for a while, but the bank failed in 1857 with serious financial consequences. Sherman next tried a legal career and moved to Kansas where he formed a partnership with two of the Ewing brothers. But Sherman had little aptitude for law, and he left the profession after losing his only case.

He fared better in the next career, accepting the superintendent's position at a military college in Louisiana that was the forerunner to Louisiana State University. Between 1859 and 1861 he served happily in the job and developed an affection for the people of the South. The feeling was apparently reciprocated, for when the Civil War began he was offered a commission in the Confederate Army. But the man who later earned the undying hatred of many a Southerner rejected this offer in favor of a colonel's commission in the Union army.

After serving as a brigade commander at Bull Run, Sherman was promoted to general and sent to Kentucky, where he nearly sabotaged his burgeoning career. Always intense and high-strung, he now quarreled with superiors and the media to the point where the press openly questioned his sanity. Fortunately one of his duties involved sending troops to Grant, and the two men forged a bond. As Grant's star began to rise he became increasingly dependent on Sherman, who proved himself worthy. At the battle of Shiloh, Sherman stayed on the field despite having four horses shot out from under him and being wounded himself. Sherman played even more prominent roles in the Vicksburg and Chattanooga campaigns, and when Grant moved east as overall commander, Sherman succeeded him on the western front.

In the spring of 1864, Sherman advanced on Atlanta at about the same time that Grant began his Wilderness campaign. In a summer filled with aggressive action, he moved south and captured Atlanta on September 1. When the main Confederate army retreated to Tennessee, Sherman undertook the bold move of abandoning his lines of supply and communication and heading deeper into enemy territory. From November 15 to December 21, Sherman's 60,000-man army cut a swath through Georgia on a march to the sea.

With his troops forced to live off the land, they helped themselves to whatever they needed and destroyed everything that might be useful to the enemy. This policy, plus the actions of renegade "bummers" who sometimes went even farther, earned Sherman everlasting enmity in the south. Sherman regretted this harsh policy, but as he later famously said in a speech in Columbus, "war is all hell," and he knew his actions would hasten the end of a particularly hellish war. Sherman's presenting the city of Savannah as a Christmas gift to Lincoln also gave northern morale a major boost.

In 1865, Sherman moved north into the Carolinas to try and force the Confederate army to surrender. In February the city of Columbia, South Carolina, was nearly destroyed by fire, but it remains unknown whether this fire was started by advancing Yankees or retreating Confederates. By April the southern army had had enough and surrendered to Sherman. While he proved he could be merciless in war, Sherman was magnanimous in victory, as his surrender terms were so generous that Secretary of War Edwin Stanton overruled them.

Among generals, Sherman was now second only to Grant in public esteem and when Grant moved on to civilian success, Sherman succeeded him. He followed Grant as the second four star full general in U.S. history in 1869, and he remained commander-in-chief of the army until he retired in

73

1883. This required spending some time in Washington, a place he despised despite having been married there.

Sherman's younger brother John had a long political career that involved over 30 years in the Senate and stints as Secretary of State and Treasury. He is best known today as sponsor of the Sherman Anti-Trust Act. But William wanted nothing to do with law or politics. When there was talk of running him for President in 1884, he replied, "If nominated, I shall not run. If elected, I shall not serve." After this rejection, he retired to New York City, where he died in 1891.

Today the house where both Sherman brothers were born is a museum operated by the Fairfield Heritage Association. Nearby are other historic buildings from the same era. The home, which was built in 1811, is also a National

Historic Landmark. For information about hours and prices, contact the Sherman House Museum, 137 East Main Street, Lancaster, 43130 or call (740) 687-5891 or go to *www.shermanhouse.org.*

Philip Sheridan

The third important Union general was not born in Ohio. Philip Sheridan was born in Albany, New York in 1831 to parents who moved to Ohio when Philip was an infant. The Sheridans were part of a wave of Irish immigrants who moved westward to help build the nation's canals. The family settled in Somerset in Perry County, where young Philip got his first job as a store clerk at age fourteen. In 1848 he received an appointment to West Point.

As a cadet, Sheridan was cool and reserved, but popular. Though standing only five foot five, "Little Phil" could be feisty, and a fight with a classmate got him suspended from the academy for a year. Graduating in 1853, he entered the army as a quartermaster and was stationed in Texas and later the Pacific Northwest. Promotion was slow in the pre-Civil War army, and Sheridan was still only a lieutenant by 1861.

When the Civil War began, Sheridan was promoted but was still ordering supplies in the quartermaster corps. It wasn't until May of 1862 that he got field command as the colonel of a Michigan cavalry regiment. He distinguished himself in combat right away and was transferred to the infantry. He continued to serve credibly at the battles of Perrysville and Stones River and was promoted to major general. He really earned Grant's respect at Missionary Ridge when

75

he led his division up a steep mountain and dislodged the Confederate army in November of 1863.

When Grant was promoted and sent to command the eastern war effort, he brought along Sheridan and installed him as head of cavalry. During Grant's Wilderness Campaign in May of 1864, Sheridan led a raid around the Confederate army that resulted in destruction of valuable supplies and the death in battle of Confederate cavalry icon Jeb Stuart. A second raid was less successful, but Grant soon decided he needed Sheridan in another capacity.

The Shenandoah Valley of Virginia had long been a thorn in the side of the Union. Not only was it far enough north to launch an attack on Washington, but the fertile soil earned the valley a reputation as the breadbasket of the Confederacy. Resolving to end this threat, Grant sent Sheridan to this area with 48,000 troops and his first chance at independent command.

Arriving in August, Sheridan moved so cautiously at first that the Confederate commander concluded that he was facing another timid foe. But when the Confederates sent some of their troops back to Richmond, Sheridan was ready to pounce. After enthusiastically detailing his plan to Grant in great detail, Grant simply replied, "Go in." On September 19, Sheridan's army defeated the Confederates at Winchester. He followed up at Fisher's Hill three days later and cleared the valley of Confederates. He now began to demolish supplies and crops, but the rebel army had not given up. On October 19, they surprised the Union Army at Cedar Creek and began to drive them back.

Sheridan had just gotten back from consultation in Washington and was sleeping fourteen miles away when informed of the attack. Leaping on his favorite horse, Rienzi, he rode to the battle and rallied his men. This incident is depicted in T. Buchanon Read's dramatic poem, *"Sheridan's Ride,"* which tells how Sheridan snatched victory from the jaws of defeat.

After this dramatic victory, Sheridan had the valley to himself and he proceeded to make the harvest a grim one for the Confederacy. After destroying crops, barns, livestock and mills, Sheridan boasted to Grant that "a crow would have had to carry its rations if it had flown across the valley." This ruthless ravaging denied the south valuable resources and helped shorten the war. In April of 1865, Sheridan rejoined Grant and played a major role in cornering Lee's Army and forcing its surrender.

Immediately afterwards, Sheridan was sent to Texas where border troubles with Mexico were brewing. He then served as military governor of Texas and Louisiana, but his policies were so harsh that he was recalled. He spent time in Europe as an observer of the Franco-Prussian War in 1870, but was mainly involved in coordinating Indian warfare in the west. In 1875, the 45-year-old Sheridan married a 23-year-old daughter of a colleague, and this late union produced four children. Sheridan succeeded Sherman as commander of the U.S. Army in 1884, and four years later was promoted to full general. The first three four star generals the army had were all raised in Ohio. Sheridan did not enjoy his new rank for long, however, as he died later that year at 57.

The local high school in nearby Thornville is named for Sheridan, but most notable monument to Sheridan is right in the center of Somerset. At the traffic circle where Routes 22 and 13 intersect is a life-sized statue of Sheridan astride Rienzi. A few blocks south of this, a plaque marks the house Sheridan had built for his parents. The citizens of Somerset have not forgotten Sheridan's horse, either, as they have named a street after Rienzi. The remains of this noble horse are stuffed and on display at the Smithsonian Institution. For more information on Sheridan's local legacy, contact the Perry County Historical Society, 105 South Columbus Street, Box 746, Somerset, 43783-0746, or go to *www.netpluscom.com/~pchs/.*

George Armstrong Custer

In addition to producing three of the most important generals in the Union army, Ohio also gave the nation George Armstrong Custer, one of the controversial and colorful military leaders in American history. Custer was born in New Rumley in Harrison County on December 5, 1839, the eldest child of a blacksmith. After the age of ten, he also lived part time with a half sister in Monroe, Michigan, which is where he met his beloved wife, Elizabeth "Libbie" Bacon. But he also spent much of his boyhood in New Rumley, where he got a reputation as a prankster who was also ambitious if not hard working.

He was bright enough to earn an appointment to West Point in 1857, although he did not excel there academically. In fact, his grades ranked him last of 34 in the class of 1861, but with the Civil War in progress he wasted little time in showing the irrelevancy of his grades. Custer joined the cavalry on the day of the Battle of Bull Run and fought in nearly every battle with the Army of the Potomac. Custer advanced through the ranks both by impressing superior officers and aggressive action in battle, and right before Gettysburg he became a general at the age of 23.

The South had a cavalry advantage early in the war, as the region was a breeding ground for both horses and horsemen. But as the war dragged on, the chivalrous notions of war faded away as irreplaceable horses and riders died off. At the same time, younger and more aggressive cavalry leaders rose through the Union ranks. Custer was a prime example of this, and his bold, flamboyant style earned praise for the man referred to by an adoring press as The Boy General.

Custer drove his men hard and was eager for any dangerous job. He earned the admiration of Sheridan, who installed Custer as commander of a cavalry division in his Shenandoah Valley campaign. In the spring of 1865, Custer played a major role in trapping Lee's army and forcing it to surrender. At the conclusion of the Appomattox campaign, Custer was promoted to the rank of major general at the age of 25.

His benefactor Sheridan had still been a lieutenant eight years after graduating from West Point, while Custer became a two star general in half that time. This was due to the needs of a wartime army that requires many more soldiers and officers of higher rank to command them. Now, with the end of the Civil War, the reverse was true, and a peacetime army meant lesser rank for all who chose to remain in the service. Custer found himself reverting all the way to the lowly rank of captain in the regular army. He further damaged his career by getting court-martialed for abandoning his troops to visit his wife.

After a one-year suspension, Custer returned to duty as Lieutenant Colonel in command of the 7th Cavalry regiment. Assigned to Indian campaigns on the Great Plains, he sought to recoup his military glory. In 1868 he led a successful attack on a Cheyenne village on Oklahoma's Washita River, although most of the casualties were women and children. While some generals like Sherman hated the press, Custer cultivated a relationship with the media and his successes got good coverage.

Custer also made good copy. He dressed in buckskin and he grew his yellow hair long and even wore it in curly ringlets. And while he had a reputation as a big game hunter, he also enjoyed musical and theatrical performances. He and Libbie had no children, but she joined him at isolated out-posts, and Custer also had various brothers and nephews join him in both military and civilian roles.

In 1874, Custer led an expedition into the Black Hills of South Dakota. Reporters that Custer had allowed along wrote of the discovery of gold, which led to a gold rush and the establishment of places like Deadwood. But this was on land previously claimed by the Sioux and an influx of sudden settlement inevitably led to more Indian warfare. In 1876, the army planned a three-pronged assault on the Sioux. Custer had originally been slated to lead one of these columns, but he had angered President Grant by testifying against Grant's Secretary of War in a government contract scandal. Now along in a subordinate role, Custer's orders were to get be-hind Indian lines and block their path of retreat.

But when he found out where the enemy was, Custer resolved to attack immediately. He may have been eager to replicate his Washita success, which had convinced him that Indians were not fierce fighters. Attacking recklessly without reconnoitering had worked well for him in the past, when his forces had more men and better supplies than his foe. But now Custer had stumbled into an extremely large concentra-tion of Indians, who had over 2,000 warriors against the 600 men of the 7th Cavalry. Worse, Custer divided his forces and personally led just 200 men on the main attack. The result was that on June 25, 1876, Custer and his entire detachment were wiped out at the Little Bighorn River. Custer's Last Stand made him a more glorious figure in death than in life.

Today, the Ohio Historical Society maintains a pavilion in New Rumley devoted to Custer. Located across the street from the church where Custer's parents were married, the site features a life-sized statue of Custer and displays concerning his life. Also, the Custer Center is open by appointment, located in a former church. To arrange a viewing of the museum, call (740) 945-5215 or (740) 945-6415 or go to *www.ohiohistory.com/places/custer.*

81

The Fighting McCooks

In addition to the most important generals in the Union Army, Ohio also produced the most significant family of generals. The Fighting McCooks were an eastern Ohio family with a prolific record. The family of Daniel McCook of Carrollton produced four sons who became generals, and three other sons plus the patriarch were officers. Four members of this clan were killed in the war. In addition, Daniel's brother John had two sons who attained the rank of general and three more who served as officers.

While the military record of all the McCooks is well known, there are some other significant aspects of the clan that are rarely noted. In an era when formal education was usually brief, the McCooks tried to provide a college education for all the children of both the "Tribe of Dan" and the "Tribe of John." And it is impressive what diverse fields that these educated leaders found success in, both before and after their military service.

The father of Daniel and John McCook emigrated from Scotland in the late 1700s and settled in the Pittsburgh area. Both sons moved westward also, a trend continued by several of their sons. Daniel, a lawyer, moved to Ohio in 1826, and John, a doctor, followed later. Daniel McCook wound up in Carrollton, where he built a house in 1837 on the public square near the Carroll County courthouse. Daniel and his wife Martha required a large house, as they produced nine sons between 1820 and 1845. When the Civil War began, all eight surviving sons plus their father volunteered for service.

Alexander McDowell McCook was the only son to make the military a career. He graduated from West Point in 1852 and served in the west fighting Indians until the war

82

began. He fought at Bull Run and Shiloh and was a major general commanding a corps at Perryville, Stone's River and Chickamauga. After the war he served on the western frontier until he retired in 1894. He was the U.S. representative at the coronation of Czar Nicholas II of Russia in 1896, and he was the only member of the Tribe of Dan to live past the age of 70.

Robert Latimer McCook became a lawyer in Cincinnati before the war. In 1861 he organized a regiment and fought in West Virginia and Kentucky. A hard fighter who was also popular with his men, he rose to the rank of brigadier general. On August 6, 1862 he was wounded and in a hospital wagon when it was overtaken by a Confederate partisan band who shot and killed him when they discovered his rank.

Daniel McCook, Junior, was also a lawyer. He relocated to Kansas in the 1850's and formed a law partnership with William Sherman and two sons of Senator Thomas Ewing (see page 72). All four partners became generals, although Daniel was one only briefly. While serving as a colonel at the Battle of Kenesaw Mountain, he was mortally wounded while gallantly leading a successful charge. He was promoted to brigadier general on July 16, 1864 and died the next day.

Edwin Stanton McCook was a graduate of the Naval Academy at Annapolis but he switched to the army during the war. He was wounded at Fort Donelson and got as high as major general. After the war he served as Governor of Dakota Territory, where he was assassinated while presiding at a public meeting in 1873.

George Wythe McCook was offered a general's commission but turned it down due to ill health. A graduate of Ohio University, he was a lawyer and a partner of Edwin

Stanton in Steubenville. During the Mexican War he commanded a regiment, but in the Civil War he confined his efforts to recruiting and served as a colonel. After the war he served as Attorney General for the state of Ohio and ran for Governor in 1871.

John J. McCook, the youngest son of Daniel, enlisted in the army as a private at age 16. He still rose to the rank of colonel and became a lawyer after the war. Latimer A. McCook, the oldest son of Daniel, followed his uncle into the medical profession. During the war he served as a surgeon, with the rank of major. Another brother, J. James McCook, had joined the navy and died at sea in 1842. And Charles Morris McCook dropped out of Kenyon College at age 19 to enlist as a private in 1861. He was killed in the Battle of Bull Run and died in the arms of his father, who had volunteered as a nurse. Daniel McCook, Senior, later entered the service at the rank of major, despite being 64 years old. While defending Ohio from Morgan's Raiders, he was mortally wounded at the Battle of Buffington Island on July 19, 1863 (see page 45).

Daniel's younger brother John served the Union cause as a volunteer surgeon until he died of illness in 1865. John's oldest son Edward Moody McCook rose to the rank of major general. After the war he served as Governor of Colorado Territory as well as minister to the Sandwich Islands (Hawaii). John's second son, Anson McCook, moved to California during the gold rush but returned and became another law partner of Stanton's. During the war he became a brigadier general and fought in many major battles. After the war he moved to New York City and served three terms in Congress. Rhoderick Sheldon McCook, another of the Tribe of John, chose a naval career. After graduating from the Naval Academy in 1859, he played a major role in the Fort Fisher campaign on the North Carolina coast. He remained in the Navy and attained the rank of commander. Another brother, Henry Christopher McCook, entered the ministry. He served as a chaplain during the war with the rank of lieutenant. In addition to his ministerial duties, he later became an expert on the behavior of ants and spiders and wrote several books on these subjects. John James McCook, the youngest son of John, also became a minister who served as a chaplain with lieutenant's rank. After the war he returned to his alma mater, Trinity College in Hartford, as a professor of modern languages.

Today, the house inhabited by the Tribe of Dan from 1837 to 1853 is a museum operated by the Ohio Historical Society and the Carroll County Historical Society. For more information on hours and fees, contact the McCook House Civil War Museum Carroll County Historical Society, Box 174, Carrollton, 44615 or call (330) 627-3345 or (800) 600-7172 or go to *www.ohiohistory.org/places/mccookhse*. There is also a monument for Daniel McCook at Buffington Island

and a family monument at Cincinnati's Spring Grove Cemetery, where several family members are buried.

One good place to view Ohio's contribution to the Civil War effort is the State House Lawn. Near the corner of High and Broad Streets is the famous "These are my jewels" statue. Life-sized depictions are of Grant, Sherman, Sheridan, generals-turned-presidents Hayes and Garfield, and Edwin Stanton of Steubenville, who served as Lincoln's Secretary of War, and Salmon P. Chase, a Cincinnati lawyer who was Lincoln's Secretary of the Treasury and then Chief Justice of the U.S. Supreme Court.

Chapter Five:
Ohio Presidents

After the Civil War, a reunited America entered into a period of unparalleled growth and prosperity. In addition to this economically gilded age, the continued subjugation of Native Americans led to the fulfillment of the promise of Manifest Destiny and emergence as a world power. As was the case in the Civil War, Ohioans had a major role in this success, both as a major swing state and as a producer of leaders.

Of the ten men elected President between 1868 and 1920, seven were born and raised in Ohio. All of them were Republicans, as eleven of fourteen Republican candidates for President during this period were born in Ohio, and in 1920 the candidates for both major parties were Ohio natives. Military service was another common thread; four of the seven were generals in the Civil War and another was a major. Another common factor was a respect for education that frequently was shown by their spouses as well.

There was, however, a great diversity in the levels and types of service that preceded their election. Grant and Taft never ran for major public office until their successful Presidential campaigns, and Harrison's and Harding's national service consisted of but a single term in the Senate. At the other end of the spectrum, Hayes and McKinley served multiple terms both as Congressmen and Governor, and Garfield served nine terms in the House of Representatives.

One thing they all had in common, in addition to an affinity for policy and people pleasing, was being the right man in the right place at the right time, and in many cases, being the least objectionable alternative. The Ohio born Presidents served with varying degrees of success, but only Virginia has sent more natives to the White House. Here are the Ohio born Presidents and the sites devoted to them that are open to the public.

Ulysses S. Grant

The first President who was born in Ohio was Ulysses S. Grant. The oldest of six children of Jesse and Hannah Simpson Grant, he was born on April 27, 1822 in the Clermont County village of Point Pleasant. The modest Grant home was just a few hundred yards from the Ohio River, but the family didn't remain there long. Jesse was a tanner with ambition and moved his leather business to the county seat of Georgetown the next year. Grant lived here (see page 66) until he went to West Point in 1839. After that, he never again lived in Ohio, and was elected to the Presidency as a resident of Illinois.

After graduating from West Point and serving as a military officer, Grant married Julia Dent in St. Louis in 1848. She was the sister of a West Point classmate, and another former classmate, and future foe, James Longstreet served in the wedding party. Grant was devoted to his engaging wife, and most of his bouts with excessive drinking occurred during prolonged absences from her. Julia's father felt Grant unworthy of his daughter, and after Grant resigned from the service in 1854 his lack of success seemed to confirm his fa-

88

ther-in-law's assessment. Grant was a failure in farming and real estate, and had such poor business sense that he freed a slave he'd inherited rather than sell him for a profit. It did not help that his style was informal and his appearance unkempt. By 1861, the 39-year-old Grant was a clerk in his family's leather goods store in Galena, Illinois.

But the Civil War gave this man, a failure in peacetime, the opportunity to rise to commander of the U.S. Army and preserver of the Union. In four years, the unknown Grant became the most famous man in the country, and many clamored for him to run for President. He originally showed no interest in politics, but was soon thrust into the national drama of Reconstruction.

Andrew Johnson, who became President after Lincoln's assassination, became embroiled in conflict with radical Republicans in Congress over punishment of the southern states that had seceded. Johnson wanted the popular Grant on his side, and named him Secretary of War to replace Johnson's enemy Edwin Stanton. But Grant felt he was being used and wound up supporting Johnson's impeachment, which arose out of this controversy. Grant's subsequent decision to seek the Presidency further sealed Johnson's future and Johnson refused to attend his successor's inauguration, the only President not named Adams to do so.

Grant's landslide victory in 1868 came with his slogan, "Let us have peace." But the feeling of unity at his election did not last. He started out on the wrong foot when he selected his own cabinet without consulting the party bosses who were used to having a hand in selection and whose cooperation he would need. Grant was also criticized for his ties to Jay Gould and James Fisk, two unscrupulous speculators who unsuccessfully tried to corner the gold market.

Grant's personal integrity was never in question, but this was certainly not the case for many of the people he appointed. His first term Vice President, his personal secretary and his Secretary of War were all implicated in separate major corruption scandals. Most of these scandals came to light after Grant was re-elected in 1872, and they, along with economic woes, put a damper on Grant's legacy. Domestically, President Grant was focused on expanding the frontier through Indian warfare and on Reconstruction of the former Confederacy. Federal troops were occupying the South until seceding states could be re-admitted to the Union and it was felt freed blacks' rights would be respected. His major foreign policy effort was an attempt to acquire the Dominican Republic that was rebuffed in the Senate.

By 1876, Grant was weary of the office and the nation was weary of scandal. He left office gladly and embarked on a world tour that wound up lasting two and a half years. The inquisitive Grant always enjoyed travel, and met with other world leaders in Europe, Africa and Asia. After landing in San Francisco and traveling across the United States, a re-energized Grant decided to seek a third term in 1880. He had a plurality of delegates heading into the Republican convention but no candidate was able to get a majority until compromise candidate James Garfield won on the 36th ballot. Though personally stung by the defeat, Grant agreed to campaign for Garfield. After the election, he retired to New York City, where he wrote his autobiography (see page 118).

Grant's birthplace is now open to the public, courtesy of the Ohio Historical Society. The three-room home, which was built in 1817, is furnished with period items. For information, contact Grant Birthplace State Memorial, 1591 State

Route 232, Point Pleasant, 45103 or call (513) 553-4911 or go to *www.ohiohistory.org/places/grantbir.*

Rutherford B. Hayes

Rutherford B. Hayes was born on October 4, 1822 in Delaware, Ohio, to a family that was used to hard times. His mother, Sophia Birchard Hayes, had lost both her parents and two siblings before she turned 21. When she and her husband, Rutherford, moved from Vermont to Ohio in 1817, tragedy followed them when their four-year-old daughter died. Then Rutherford died of typhus while Sophia was pregnant with the son she would name for him. A final tragedy occurred in 1825 when her nine-year-old son drowned in an ice skating accident. The survivors of all this family trauma became a close-knit group. They consisted of Sophia, her daughter Fanny, her son Rutherford, and her younger brother Sardis Birchard, who became a sort of surrogate father to the children.

Education was stressed in this household, and Rud, as he was called, became a stellar student. He was sent east to Connecticut for prep school, where he excelled. Although he had New England roots, Hayes considered himself a proud Buckeye, and all his life he favored his Ohioans over easterners. He returned to Ohio to attend Kenyon College, where he was valedictorian, and then he went back east to Harvard Law School. Upon graduation, he moved to Lower Sandusky, as Fremont was then called, where his uncle Sardis was prospering.

However, Hayes found that Fremont did not offer enough business or stimulation for him, and he relocated to

Cincinnati in 1849. Here he fell in love with Lucy Webb, a lively doctor's daughter from Chillicothe. They were married in 1852 and came to have eight children. Hayes did equally well in business, as his law practice thrived in the bustling city. He became involved in some slavery cases that got him interested in the anti-slavery beliefs of the newly formed Republican Party. In 1858 he was named city solicitor and was in the office when the Civil War started.

He enlisted when the war began and was soon made a colonel in command of the 23rd Ohio regiment. Hayes was as devoted to his men as they were to him and he regularly praised Ohio troops over those from eastern states. He was wounded at South Mountain right before the Battle of Antietam, but he returned but he returned to command and to Ohio to help defeat Morgan's Raiders (see page 43). While serving with Sheridan in the Shenandoah Valley in 1864 he was promoted to brigadier general and by the war's end he was a major general.

While serving in the army, Hayes had gotten elected to Congress, but he did not take office until the war was over. He disliked serving in Washington, and in 1867 he returned home to be elected Governor of Ohio, defeating William Howard Taft's father for the nomination. During his two terms he got Ohio to ratify the 14th and 15th amendments granting blacks civil liberties and established Ohio State University. He then tried to retire to Spiegel Grove, the elegant home in Fremont that he'd inherited from Sardis Birchard. But he came back in 1875 to win a third term as Governor.

The Republican Party convention was held in Cincinnati in 1876 and Hayes attended as governor of the host state, but wound up becoming his party's nominee for President.

92

Grant's retirement left a wide-open field of contenders, and when none could get a majority, Hayes was picked as a compromise candidate on the 7th ballot. Hayes was counted on to deliver Ohio's electoral votes, but he generally ran a low-key campaign. One significant aspect of his platform was a promise to serve only one term.

Hayes lost the popular vote to Democrat Samuel Tilden, but Tilden had only 184 electoral votes, one short of what was needed. This was because the election in three southern states was in dispute, with a total of twenty electoral votes held in limbo. The bitter controversy continued up to the eve of inauguration day, when a panel voted along party lines to give all twenty votes, and the Presidency, to Hayes. As a compromise, the Republicans agreed to withdraw all Federal troops from the South, where they had been safeguarding the rights of freed slaves. This deal to gain four more years of White House control led to brutal suppression of southern blacks' voting rights by southern whites and to Democratic control of the South for the next 90 years.

Though he was ridiculed as His Fraudulency, Hayes worked effectively as a cautious pragmatist with the Democratic-controlled Congress. Although he moved slowly on civil service reform, he did set in motion events that helped replace the spoils system in government employment. Hayes described his style as "radical in thought, conservative in method," although after he left office he was more vocal in favor of reform.

What is most remembered about the Hayes White House was an alcohol ban imposed by his wife, who came to be known as Lemonade Lucy. In addition to her advocacy of temperance, Lucy was the first college graduate First Lady. She was also the first First Lady to be referred to as such.

93

Hayes enjoyed moderate success as President, but he kept his promise to serve only a single term. He retired to Spiegel Grove in 1881 and devoted his final years to his family and speaking out on public issues. When he died in 1893, his funeral was attended not only by the current President, Cleveland, but also by the next President, William McKinley, who had served with Hayes in the 23rd Ohio.

While the house where Hayes was born was torn down in 1928, Spiegel Grove is now a major tourist attraction. Rutherford and Lucy are buried on the grounds, and the Ohio Historical Society offers tours of the 33-room mansion. Right next door is the Hayes Presidential Library, the first presidential library to be built. For more information, contact the Rutherford B. Hayes Presidential Center, 1337 Hayes Ave., Fremont, 43420-2796, or call (419) 332-2081 or (800) 998-7737 or go to *www.rbhayes.org*. Lucy Webb Hayes' birthplace is also open for tours. To find out more, contact Friends of Lucy Hayes Heritage Center, 90 W. Sixth Street, Box 1790, Chillicothe, 45601 or call (614) 775-5829.

James A. Garfield

James A. Garfield was the last President to be born in a log cabin, but he saw no advantage in his humble roots, saying, "I lament sorely I was born to poverty... let no man praise me because I was born poor... it was very bad for my life." Garfield was born November 19, 1831 in the Cuyahoga County village of Orange. His father was a canal worker who died when James was only two. James inherited his father's strength and wound up working along the canals himself in his youth.

Yet he also had more academic talents. He was so comfortable at public speaking that he became a lay preacher and contemplated a career in the ministry. But his real passion was learning and he headed toward an academic life. At seventeen he attended Hiram Eclectic Institute, the forerunner to Hiram College. There he excelled as a student so much that he wound up teaching classes. At age 23 he went to Williams College in Massachusetts to complete his degree.

He came under the tutelage of college president Mark Hopkins, and came to increase his respect for education and in particular the importance of teachers. He later said, "the ideal college consists of Mark Hopkins on one end of a log and a student on the other." After graduating in 1856, he returned to become a teacher at Hiram. In 1858, he married fellow teacher Lucretia Randolph, a daughter of one of the Institute's founders. His marriage to "Crete," as he called her, foundered at first but eventually grew into a solid union.

In 1860, Garfield was elected to the state senate, but his service was interrupted by the Civil War. He enlisted and was made colonel of the 42nd Ohio regiment. He got a taste of independent command when he led his troops to victory in a skirmish in Kentucky, and was promoted to general and commanded a brigade at Shiloh. Later he served as chief of staff for fellow Ohioan William Rosecrans at the Battle of Chickamauga.

Garfield was elected to Congress in 1863 and left the army. He wound up serving nine terms in the House and developed a good reputation there. As a Congressman, he was likable and accommodating, and eager to compromise. He came to specialize in economic matters, and was influenced by fellow Ohioan Salmon P. Chase to adhere to the gold standard and pursue conservative fiscal policies. He served as chair of the powerful Ways and Means committee and became minority leader in 1874.

By 1880, Garfield was ready for a change, and he was elected to the Senate for a term to begin in 1881. In those days, Senators were elected by the state legislatures, and Garfield accepted his new posting with strings attached. A part of this was agreeing to support the Presidential candidacy of John Sherman, a former Senator from Ohio, and the brother of General Sherman. Garfield went to the Republican convention in Chicago as a delegate pledged to Sherman, who was in a wide-open fight for the nomination due to Hayes retiring after one term. But no candidate was able to get a delegate majority and Garfield emerged as a compromise candidate who won on the 36th ballot.

Garfield ran his campaign from the large home he had purchased in Mentor in 1876. He added onto the home, which the press named Lawnfield, due to the large lawn surrounding the house. Garfield won the popular vote by just 10,000 votes out of nine million cast, although his electoral vote margin was larger. This put Garfield in the unique position of being a sitting Congressman, a Senator-elect, and the President-elect. But as the Senate and Presidential terms were to begin the day his Congressional term expired, he resigned his Senate seat without serving and accepted the Presidency.

No one knows what kind of President Garfield might have become because he was shot just four months into his term. His killer was a deranged office seeker disappointed at not being named Consul to France. Garfield was shot in Washington on July 2, 1881 but he lived until September 19. The cause of his death was not the bullet wound itself but the infection from probes with unsterilized tools. The nation mourned the untimely death of its President and Garfield lay on display at the Capitol Rotunda. His body then rode a funeral train to Cleveland, where 150,000 people viewed it on Public Square. The body was then taken down Euclid Avenue for interment in Cleveland's prestigious Lake View Cemetery.

Garfield's birthplace is open for visitation year round. For information, contact the Moreland Hills Historical Society, 38230 Chagrin Boulevard, Moreland Hills, 44022-1211 or call (440) 247-7282 or go to *www.morelandhills.com*. Lawnfield is a National Historic Site operated in conjunction with the Western Reserve Historical Society. The eight-acre site includes the 29-room house, visitor center, museum and library, and various outbuildings. For more information, contact the James A. Garfield National Historic Site, 8095 Mentor Ave., Mentor, 44060-5753 or call (440) 255-8722 or go to *www.nps.gov/jaga/* or *www.wrhs.org*.

Benjamin Harrison

Ohio and Virginia have been engaged in a competition over which state has produced the most Presidents. The answer depends on how you decide what state someone is "from". The first person elected President while a resident of Ohio was William Henry Harrison in 1840, but Harrison was born and raised in Virginia and didn't come to Ohio until he was nineteen. If Ohio claims Harrison, then it must forfeit claims to Grant, who left Ohio at seventeen and was elected from Illinois, and to Benjamin Harrison, who moved to Indiana at age 21. The definition chosen for this book is birth, so the Harrison that counts here is Benjamin.

But they are closely connected, as William Henry Harrison was the grandfather of Benjamin Harrison, who was born in his grandfather's home at North Bend in Hamilton County on August 20, 1833. The illustrious Harrison clan produced more than just two Presidents. William Henry Harrison's father was a signer of the Declaration of Independence. His son, John Scott Harrison, was a Congressman, although he is best known today as a trivia answer as the only man who is both a father and a son of a President. Though born on his grandfather's estate, Benjamin was raised nearby where the Great Miami and Ohio River meet. He grew up in a traditional environment where religion and education were stressed. As their rural area had little in the way of schools, Harrison was sent to Cincinnati to study at Cary's Academy. From there, he went on to Miami University, where he ranked third in his class of 1852. The next year he married Caroline Scott, the daughter of a professor. Harrison had considered a career in the ministry, but decided a law career would be a better way to support a family. He studied in Cincinnati, and was admitted to the bar in 1854.

Harrison could have stayed and taken advantage of his family connections, but he soon moved to Indianapolis. Rejecting his family credentials, he announced in Indiana that, "I want it understood that I am the grandson of nobody. I believe that every man should stand on his own merits." In his efforts to establish a legal practice, he became involved with the newly formed Republican Party, and was soon named Indianapolis city attorney. He was reluctant to surrender such a lucrative post when the Civil War began, but in 1862 he recruited a regiment and was named colonel of the 70th Indiana. His unit saw mainly camp duty until they joined Sherman's army in the Atlanta campaign in 1864. Harrison acquitted himself well in combat and was promoted to general in 1865 before returning to his law practice after the war.

Deeply religious and patriotic, though also considered cold and aloof, Harrison was a good speaker whose gravitations toward politics seemed natural. He ran for governor of Indiana in 1876 but lost. In 1880 he attended the Republican convention as a delegate and was one of the early supporters of Garfield's candidacy. Backing the right man can lead to rewards, and in 1881 the Indiana legislature picked Harrison for a seat in the U.S. Senate. He distinguished himself in his single term, particularly after Democrat Grover Cleveland was elected President in 1884. As a leader of the opposition, Harrison became one of Cleveland's most visible critics, and in 1888, he became the Republican nominee for President, in part due to Indiana's status as a swing state.

During the campaign he got help from another former Union general, Lew Wallace, who was the brother of Harrison's law partner. Wallace is best known as the author of the novel *Ben Hur*, but he also wrote Harrison's campaign biography. Harrison ran his campaign from his front porch against the incumbent Cleveland and the race was close. Though Cleveland narrowly won the popular vote, Harrison won an electoral majority and became the first person to defeat a sitting president since his grandfather in 1840. Four years later, Cleveland became the second man since 1840 to perform this feat, and in doing so, became the only person to win the popular vote for President exactly three times.

During Harrison's term, the Indian wars were concluded and six new states were added, bringing to Congress twelve new Senators and seven new Congressmen—all Republicans. Despite this, Harrison's support of high protective tariffs led to price increases that led to a midterm takeover of Congress by the Democrats. Harrison was re-nominated by his party but lost a rematch to Cleveland in 1892. Worse yet, Caroline died just before the election.

In retirement, this paragon of rectitude caused a minor scandal when he remarried to his wife's niece, who was younger than his own children, who disapproved of the marriage. He fathered a child from this union that was younger than all his grandchildren. Harrison also continued his law practice, wrote books and articles, and became involved in international law. He died in his home in Indianapolis on March 13, 1901.

There is no monument to Benjamin Harrison in Ohio, although his Indianapolis home is a museum. The North Bend house he was born in burned in 1855 and the house he grew up in was torn down in 1959. But there is one President Harrison monument located at his birth site. The tomb of William Henry Harrison and his wife is at North Bend on Cliff Road fifteen miles downtown from Cincinnati overlooking the Ohio River. For more information, contact Site Operations Department, Ohio Historical Society, 1982 Velma Ave., Columbus, 43211 or call (513) 297-2630 or (800) 686-1535 or go to *www.ohiohistory.org/places/harrison/*.

William McKinley

William McKinley was born in the Trumbull County city of Niles on January 29, 1843. He was the seventh of nine children, and his father was an employee of an iron foundry who later became a small businessman. The family stressed education and soon moved to nearby Poland to take advantage of a Methodist-run high school there. William was close to his mother and his older sister Anna, who funded her brother's foray into college at Allegheny College in Meadville, Pennsylvania. But, the workload and expenses proved to be too much for the seventeen-year-old. He returned home and taught in a rural school and worked in the post office until 1861.

101

When the Civil War began, McKinley enlisted as a private in the 23rd Ohio regiment. But his commanding officer, Rutherford Hayes, saw potential in the teenager and he was promoted to commissary sergeant. During the bloody battle of Antietam, McKinley brought a wagon full of sandwiches and coffee to the men while under heavy fire. Shortly afterwards, he was made an officer, and he rose to the rank of major by the end of the war while only 22 years old.

Returning home, he decided on a law career and apprenticed with a firm in Youngstown before going to law school in Albany, New York. He was admitted to the Ohio bar in Warren, and then moved to Canton where his sister Anna taught school. In Canton, he fell in love with Ida Saxton, the beautiful and pampered daughter of a prominent banker. They were married in 1871 and the couple had two daughters in the next two years. But in a short period, both daughters and Ida's mother died, and she never quite recovered from this. She suffered migraines and epileptic fits and became a semi-invalid the rest of her life. McKinley remained devoted to his needy wife and accepted his lot stoically as he did everything else.

The personable McKinley prospered in his practice and soon became involved in politics. He campaigned for Hayes for governor in 1867 and served a term as Stark County Prosecutor. In 1877, McKinley was elected to Congress, and except for one term, remained there until 1891. As a Congressman, he was a moderate in a swing district who focused his efforts on monetary issues. In particular, he championed a high tariff to protect the sale of U.S. goods. In 1890, he sponsored the McKinley Tariff, but the result of this was high prices that cost many jobs, including McKinley's, when he was defeated for re-election.

Undaunted, he ran for Governor of Ohio and won two terms, gaining valuable experience in the executive branch. An economic downturn in 1893 led to layoffs and labor strife, but he managed both effectively. As governor, he also campaigned tirelessly for other Republican candidates, which helped his status in the party. But what really made him Presidential timbre was an alliance with Cleveland-based political boss Marc Hanna, a partnership that got McKinley the nomination in 1896. While some like Theodore Roosevelt grumbled that Hanna advertised McKinley as though he were a patent medicine, this approach was effective.

McKinley conducted a front porch campaign from his Canton home, in contrast to the frenetic whistle stops of Democratic candidate William Jennings Bryan. Bryan got attention for his colorful speeches, but McKinley won big, and was the first President since Grant to win a majority of all votes cast.

As a Congressman, McKinley's tariff policy was isolationist, but as President the nation entered into world affairs, mainly due to the Spanish-American War. At this time, Cuban insurgents were rebelling against their harsh Spanish colonial masters. The U.S. Battleship *Maine* was sent to Havana to protect American interests, and when it was blown up on February 15, 1898, the Spanish were blamed. The press had more to do with going to war than McKinley, but in six months the navy had established the U.S. as a world power- and a colonial power as well, as the country received Guam, Puerto Rico and the Philippines from Spain, while Cuba got independence.

A war victory and strong economy gave McKinley an easy re-election victory in a 1900 rematch with Bryan- but he did not get much of a second term. He was assassinated by an

103

anarchist in Buffalo in September of 1901. Considerate to the end, while being taken to an ambulance he asked that his shooter not be harmed, and to be careful in giving his wife the news. McKinley died of gangrene on September 14th, and was interred in an ornate memorial in Canton dedicated in 1907.

Next door to the McKinley Memorial is the McKinley Presidential Library, which is operated by the Stark County Historical Society. For more information, contact the McKinley Museum, 800 McKinley Monument Drive NW, Box 20070, Canton, 44701-0070, or call (330) 455-7043. McKinley's birthplace in Niles is commemorated at the McKinley Public Library, 40 N. Main Street, Niles, 44446-5004, phone (330) 652-1704, or visit *www.mckinley.lib.oh.us.*

The McKinleys' Canton home is now restored as the First Ladies National Historic Site. Ida Saxton McKinley's home at 331 Market Avenue South is as it was during her time but also features exhibits pertaining to all first ladies. A block away at 205 Market Avenue South is the Education and Research Center, which includes a First Ladies research library. For more information, contact the First Ladies National Historic Site, 331 Market Avenue South, Canton, 44702-2701 or call (330) 452-0876 or go to *www.firstladies.org.*

William Howard Taft

William Howard Taft was the most prominent member of the most prominent political dynasty in Ohio history. His father served as Grant's Secretary of War, his son and grandson were U.S. Senators from Ohio, and his great-grandson was a two-term Governor of Ohio. But no one in this lineage loomed larger, literally or figuratively, than 300-pound William Howard Taft, the only man in U.S. history to serve as both President and Chief Justice of the Supreme Court.

Taft was born in Cincinnati on September 15, 1857, the seventh child of ten born to Alphonse Taft, a transplanted New England lawyer. Success was expected from his patrician roots, and Taft was salutatorian of his class at Woodward High School. He then went to Yale, his father's alma mater, where he also finished second in his class. Next, he returned home to attend law school, and he was admitted to the bar in 1880. Though he was made assistant district attorney and city solicitor, Taft didn't consider the law as an entry into politics, but as the ultimate career.

His wife was the one who had political savvy. In 1886, Taft married Helen Herren, whose father was a judge and had been Rutherford Hayes' law partner. Nellie, as she was

105

called, was college educated, bright, lively and ambitious. Taft was made a judge in 1887 and might have remained a local judge had he not had such an ambitious spouse. Urged to lobby for a Supreme Court nomination, Taft was still young but in 1890 President Harrison named him U.S. Solicitor General, which meant he was responsible for arguing the government's case before the Supreme Court. He won fifteen of seventeen cases before being placed on the U.S. Federal Circuit Court in 1892. This meant a return to Cincinnati, so Taft also became Dean of the Cincinnati Law School in addition to his judicial duties.

Taft was a big, congenial self-effacing man who hated conflict. He was also an earnest, hard-working model of integrity whose lack of personal ambition made him nonthreatening to politicians. In 1900, President McKinley offered Taft the job of head of the commission governing the Philippines, which had been won from Spain in the Spanish-American War. He protested he was unqualified, but was persuaded to accept the post. With his usual hard work, he dealt with the insurgency there and made strides in winning the hearts and minds of the Filipinos. Nellie liked being the wife of the colonial governor. She made the palace a hub of social activity and also traveled widely.

In 1904, Taft was summoned home by President Theodore Roosevelt and offered his father's old post of Secretary of War. He became the workhorse of the Cabinet, and Roosevelt gave increasing responsibility to his most trusted aide. Roosevelt had made a campaign promise to not seek re-election in 1908, and as others clamored for his mantle, he chose to anoint the quieter Taft as his successor. Taft resisted, saying, "Politics, when I am in it, makes me sick," but he was powerless to resist the strong wills of Roosevelt and

Nellie. In his first run for any political office, other than one campaign for a local judgeship, Taft was elected President with two-thirds of the popular and electoral votes.

As President, Taft experienced failure for the first time. His hatred of conflict caused him to defer to Congress, and he frequently fled Washington for extensive travel junkets. This led to media criticism, and, for a large-boned man, Taft had a thin skin, and he brooded over his treatment. However, Nellie enjoyed being first lady and was busied herself hosting parties, redecorating the White House and trying to get the servants to wear uniforms. She also imported the Japanese cherry trees that brighten Washington every spring.

Taft continued the Roosevelt policy of trust busting, or breaking up monopolies, but when Roosevelt returned from a lengthy African safari, he was not satisfied. By the time Taft fired his friend Gifford Pinchot as Secretary of the Interior, Roosevelt had decided he wanted his old job back. He opposed Taft for the nomination in 1912, but the party did not abandon the incumbent and re-nominated Taft. Roosevelt then ran as a third-party candidate, which guaranteed a victory for Democratic candidate Woodrow Wilson. In his third run for public office, Taft got only eight electoral votes and became the only incumbent running for re-election to finish third.

The Tafts then moved to Connecticut, where he became a law professor at Yale, which improved his temperament considerably. But in 1921, President Harding offered him the position of Chief Justice of the U.S. Supreme Court, the one job he had wanted all along. He served happily in this job until 1930, and died just one month after retiring. As befits one of only two men to head two of the three branches of the federal government (James Polk was the other), Taft was bur-

ied in Arlington National Cemetery, the only President besides Kennedy to be buried there.

The home where Taft was born and raised is now a National Historic Site open to the public for daily tours. For information, contact the William Howard Taft National Historic Site, 2038 Auburn Avenue, Cincinnati, 45219-3025 or
call (513) 684-3263 or go to *www.nps.gov/wiho.*

Warren G. Harding

Warren G. Harding was born in the Morrow County
village of Corsica, now called Blooming Grove, on November 2, 1865. He was the oldest of eight children born to a
homeopathic physician and business speculator whose
schemes never quite panned out. The family later moved
across the Marion County line to Caledonia. Harding went to
Ohio Central College in Iberia, where he played cornet and

worked on the college paper. After graduating, he moved to the county seat of Marion and was briefly engaged in teaching and the insurance business.

In 1884 he bought a weekly newspaper called the *Marion Star* and found his calling. Through knack and hard work he transformed the failing paper into a profitable daily and established himself as a civic leader. In searching for a suitable bride he found Florence King De Wolfe, a college educated daughter of a banker. She was also five years older than Harding and a divorcee with a son. She supported herself giving piano lessons, but after marrying Harding, this woman referred to as the Duchess rose to First lady.

Harding the newspaper publisher eventually branched into politics, and in 1899 he was elected to the Ohio Senate as a Republican in a heavily Democratic county. He aspired to the governor's job but in 1904 was convinced by Republican Party leaders to settle for a term as lieutenant governor. He ran for governor in 1910 but lost, though he showed himself to be a personable and effective campaigner.

In 1913, direct popular election to the U.S. Senate was established, and Harding the next year became Ohio's first popularly elected Senator. Serving in the Senate during the World War I years, he was not particularly active; in fact, he missed 43% of roll call votes. But he still made a favorable impression, as the sort of non-intellectual civic booster who personified his time. He played major roles in the Republican National Conventions in 1912 and 1916 and had already expressed an interest in the Presidency as 1920 approached.

He helped his cause with an alliance with political operative Harry Daugherty, a native of Washington Court House. Serving as campaign manager, Daugherty predicted Harding would emerge from the proverbial smoke-filled room as a compromise candidate, and that's what happened after ten ballots. Like some other Ohio candidates, Harding was the least objectionable of second-tier candidates in a race lacking a clear favorite.

His opponent was another Ohio newspaperman turned politician, Governor James Cox of Dayton. Harding head-quartered his campaign from the front porch of his Marion home. He stressed an isolationist "America First" platform and advocated a "Return to Normalcy" from the tumult of World War I. The fact that women could now vote was sup-posedly also in the handsome Harding's favor. He was elected President by a large margin on his 55th birthday.

Harding was another Ohio President who was an ac-commodator not eager to take firm stands. As a brewery in-vestor who supported Prohibition, he liked to have it both ways. Harding preferred people to policy, but some of the people he surrounded himself with served him poorly. To-ward the end of his Presidency, he began to realize the extent of the corruption of some of his appointees, and he lamented, "I can take care of my enemies all right, but my damn friends...they're the ones keeping me walking the floor nights!"

The biggest scandal of the Harding Presidency was the Teapot Dome, where his Secretary of the Interior got caught selling oil leases and became the first cabinet officer to go to prison. His equally corrupt head of the Veteran's Bureau also went to prison. Daugherty, who Harding had made Attorney General despite a lack of qualifications, was a leading figure in what came to be called the Ohio Gang. Daugherty was in-dicted, but escaped conviction after invoking the 5th Amend-ment, though a close associate committed suicide after being implicated.

These scandals were just coming to the surface when Harding embarked on a western trip in the summer of 1923. He became ill on the west coast and died in San Francisco on August 2, but the exact cause of death has been debated. The death of the President caused much mourning at first, but the exposure of new scandals quickly tarnished his legacy, and Harding is considered today to be one of the worst Presidents. In addition to corruption trials, there were rumors Harding had been poisoned, and then a former mistress wrote a book about her affair with Harding and their love child. Harding's reputation sank so low that his successor Calvin Coolidge was not willing to come to Marion to dedicate Harding's tomb.

President Hoover did dedicate the tomb in 1931, and it is an impressive monument located at State Route 423 and Vernon Heights Boulevard in Marion. Located on a ten-acre park, it is free and open year round in daylight hours. Harding's home in maintained by the Ohio Historical Society. The house, which Harding had built in 1891, contains original

111

furnishings and an adjacent press house serves as a museum. For more information, contact the Harding Home State Memorial, 380 Mount Vernon Avenue, Marion, 43302, or call (740) 387-9630 or (800) 600-6894, or go to *www.ohiohistory.org/places/harding.*

Chapter Six:
Arts and Sciences

Although no Ohioan has occupied the White House since 1923, the state has nonetheless produced many nationally significant figures since that time- and before. Worthy of particular note are Ohioans' accomplishments in the areas of both arts and sciences. Ohio natives have always made contributions in many of the arts, but most noticeably in literature, which is highlighted at historical sites devoted to individual Ohio authors. In the realm of science, Ohioans have inaugurated many developments that have had major industrial consequences, particularly in aviation. Here are some sites devoted to notable Ohioans in these fields.

Arts

Ohio natives have contributed to music from the time of *"Dixie"* composer Daniel Decatur Emmet and Benjamin Hanby (see page 55) to the present Ohio-based inductees in Cleveland's Rock and Roll Hall of Fame. Ohio has also produced nationally-known painters since Hudson River School founder Thomas Cole began his career in Steubenville in the 1820s. George Bellows, a leading figure in the Ash Can School, was a native of Columbus. And Cincinnati was the center of a major artistic scene that included painters George Duveneck, Worthington Whittredge, Lily Martin Spencer and Robert Duncanson - one of the first black men to make a living as an artist. In the performing arts, Ohio has produced such notables as Annie Oakley, Lillian Gish, Clark Gable and Bob Hope, as well as many current figures who are still actively making names for themselves.

But it is in literature that Ohioans have had the most dramatic impact, and this is reflected in the number of museums and sites devoted to Ohio authors. Ohio authors are so plentiful that a small city like Martin's Ferry in Belmont County produced two literary lions in novelist William Dean Howells and poet James Wright. Even smaller locales produced the genius of Sherwood Anderson and Ambrose Bierce. There are several Ohio sites devoted to pioneers or masters of specific genres or to nationally significant authors on books that touch on all aspects of literature.

William McGuffey

In addition to a handful of literary giants, Ohio has also produced some writers who were either pioneers or masters of specific genres. One of these is William Holmes McGuffey, whose Eclectic Reader textbooks taught Americans to read for nearly a century. He is an example of how Ohio has played a role in education since the Northwest Ordinance of 1787 stipulated that one section per township of all Ohio land be set aside for the benefit of public education.

McGuffey's Ohio nativity is subject to question, as he was born either right before or right after his parents moved here to the Northwest Territory from western Pennsylvania in 1800. But he was Ohio-raised in the recently settled town of Youngstown by poor Scots-Irish parents who were distinguished only in that his mother was literate at a time when this was rare for pioneer women. Young McGuffey displayed academic aptitude as well and was enrolled in a subscription school run by Reverend William Wick. Here he astonished his peers with his prowess, and in particular he demonstrated a prodigious memory.

So rapid was his progress that by age fourteen, he was already teaching at a rural local school. He went on to college at Washington College in Pennsylvania, but as he had to pay his own way, his progress was slowed. By 1826 he was teaching in Kentucky when he was hired by Miami University as a professor of ancient languages, and he began a 48-year college career.

McGuffey took teaching very seriously and adopted techniques similar to Horace Mann, another notable educator with strong Ohio connections. But what really distinguished McGuffey was his introduction of reading textbooks for primary grades. McGuffey's Readers not only taught children to read, but the examples he used were carefully chosen to add moral instruction to the process. These texts came to be used all across the country, and it is estimated that a phenomenal total of over 120 million copies were printed by 1920.

McGuffey's First Reader was published by the Cincinnati firm of Truman and Smith in 1836. Over the next 21 years, a total of six readers plus a speller and primer were published. McGuffey left Miami in 1836 and later served as President of Ohio University, which is Ohio's oldest college, having been chartered in 1804. In 1845, he became professor of moral philosophy at the University of Virginia, which despite its Jeffersonian connection is not as old as Ohio University. He remained at Virginia until his death in 1873, and his Readers continued to be used for years afterwards.

115

Today, Miami University maintains a McGuffey Museum in the home that McGuffey and his wife Harriet purchased in 1827. For information about hours, location and parking, contact the William Holmes McGuffey Museum, National Historic Landmark, 410 E. Spring Street, Oxford, 45056 or call (513) 529-8380 or go to *www.units.muohio.edu/mcguffeymuseum.*

Harriet Beecher Stowe

There may be no better example of the capability of a book to influence history than Harriet Beecher Stowe's *Uncle Tom's Cabin.* So great was the impact of this anti-slavery novel that when President Lincoln met the author, he was alleged to have said, "So you're the little lady who started this big war." Stowe was not an Ohio native, nor did she write her famous book here. But the eighteen years she spent living in Cincinnati gave her the background and inspiration for the novel.

Harriet Beecher was born in Litchfield, Connecticut, in 1811. She was just four when her mother died, but was well taken care of in a large and well-off family. Her father was Lyman Beecher, a noted Congregationalist minister, educator and reformer. Several of her brothers also joined the ministry, and one, Henry Ward Beecher, became almost as well known as Harriet.

Harriet attended school in Hartford, but in 1832 she accompanied her father to Cincinnati, where he had been hired to head the Lane Theological Seminary. Her sister Catherine also came along and founded a companion school, the Western Female Institute. Harriet taught here and also wrote short stories for the monthly *Western Magazine*.

In 1836, she married Calvin Stowe, a professor at Lane. Though he encouraged her writing, she had little output in the ensuing years while she bore and raised seven children. However, she did gather considerable material for future use from her interaction with Cincinnati area abolitionists. Although not as extreme as some abolitionists, Reverend Beecher was in contact with most movement leaders, and from them Harriet heard tales of the horrors of slavery. She made only a brief foray into Kentucky herself, but heard men like John Rankin of Ripley (see page 52) tell harrowing stories about slaves fleeing across the Ohio River on ice floes.

In 1850, Calvin Stowe accepted a position at Bowdoin College in Maine. After doing her research in the swirling abolitionist milieu of Cincinnati, Harriet began writing in the quiet of Maine. *Uncle Tom's Cabin* was originally published as a serial in a Washington abolitionist magazine called *The National Era*. As the final installment ran in the spring of 1852, the story was published in book form.

In putting a personal face on the tragedy of slavery, the novel played a major role in accelerating abolitionist fervor, and it was an immediate success. *Uncle Tom's Cabin* sold 10,000 copies the first week and a phenomenal 300,000 copies the first year. Though the book made the author hated in the South, she was lionized in England where the book sold 1.5 million copies. It was also translated into two dozen foreign languages. Though she wrote thirty more books and countless magazine articles before her death in 1896, nothing could approach the impact of her first novel. And while she never again lived in Ohio, her experience here was the essential part of a book that changed history.

The house where Harriet Beecher Stowe lived in Cincinnati is now a museum run by the Ohio Historical Society and contains artifacts and exhibits pertaining to the abolitionist movement of the period. To find out more, contact the Stowe House State Memorial, 2950 Gilbert Avenue, Cincinnati, 45214 or call (513) 632-5120 or go to *www.ohiohistory.org/places/stowe/*.

Ulysses S. Grant

Ulysses S. Grant has already been noted as a general (see page 66) and as a President (see page 88). But he is also worthy of note as a writer for being a pioneer practitioner of that literary form known as the Presidential memoir. Although his memoirs covered only his life through the Civil War, they achieved a great critical and commercial success. His struggle to write this book makes his story all the more heroic.

118

After winning the Civil War and serving two terms as President, Grant was entitled to a dignified and comfortable retirement, but this was denied him. After moving to New York City in 1881, Grant entered into a partnership with financier Ferdinand Ward. Grant misplaced trust in his partner, who absconded with funds and left Grant liable. After borrowing from millionaire William Vanderbilt, Grant found himself deep in debt, but was determined to pay off all creditors and provide for his wife.

Around this time, Grant wrote a few magazine articles about his war experiences that were well received. At the urging of Mark Twain, who agreed to publish, Grant resolved to try to recoup his losses by writing his memoirs. But Grant suffered another cruel blow when he was diagnosed with throat cancer. He now became consumed by a desire to complete the book before the disease could claim him. In the process he became a part of the grim tradition of the Presidential deathwatch.

As Grant coughed up blood and his voice failed, he dismissed the secretary he was dictating to and wrote his book in longhand. In July of 1885 he left the heat of the city for a cooler climate upstate. Late in the month, the nation was surprised to see a photo of Grant in a top hat calmly reading a newspaper. In a final burst of energy he had rallied and completed his manuscript on July 20. He died three days later. But he won his final battle, as his book earned $450,000, more than enough to cover his debts and enable his widow Julia to live out her life in comfort.

Grant's memoirs were praised for the same clear and straightforward style that had characterized his performance as commander-in-chief. His writing style may have been honed by his West Point education, but his last school before

119

being admitted to the military academy was at John Rankin's Academy in Ripley (see page 52). But the school where he learned to write is still standing in Georgetown and is operated by the Ohio Historical Society. For more information, contact the Grant Schoolhouse, located at 508 South Water Street, by writing to the Grant Homestead Association, 318 W. State Street, Georgetown, 45121, or call (937) 378-4222, or go to *www.ohiohistory.org/places/grantsch.*

Paul Laurence Dunbar

The first African-American to make a living as a writer was Ohio native Paul Laurence Dunbar. Despite his premature death at 33, he wrote over 500 poems and 24 books in his brief career. His pioneering efforts helped make it possible for the next generation of black authors and artists to create the Harlem Renaissance of the 1920s.

Dunbar was born in Dayton in 1872, the son of two former slaves. His father had escaped to Canada, but returned to join the Union army and fight for freedom for others of his race. The Dunbars wanted a better life for their only child, and this included an education. He was sent to Dayton Central High School, where he was the only black student in the class of 1891. One of his classmates and friends was Orrville Wright (see page 130). Dunbar thrived in school, serving as editor of the school paper and president of the literary society and also composing the class song.

Yet the only job he could get after graduating was as an elevator operator in a downtown skyscraper for four dollars a week. He started a newspaper for Dayton's black community that was printed by the Wright Brothers Printing Company, but it folded after a few issues. He also wrote poems for other newspapers, and in 1893 he self-published a collection called *Oak and Ivy*. He sold this work to his elevator passengers and began to attract patrons.

His big break came in 1895 when his book, *Majors and Minors*, got a glowing review in *Harper's Magazine* from critic and fellow Ohioan William Dean Howells. Sales boomed and Dunbar became in demand on the lecture circuit, and even toured England. He was offered a federal job as an assistant at the Library of Congress in Washington, which gave him guaranteed income and time to pursue his writing. He was briefly married to fellow poet Alice Moore, but his slow decline from tuberculosis gradually robbed him until his death in 1906.

He wrote many of his poems in dialect, where the simple language dealt with complex and deep issues. He also wrote more traditional verse, four novels and many songs, including the alma mater for Booker T. Washington's Tuskegee Institute. Today, Dunbar's house is part of the National Park Service Dayton Aviation Heritage National Historic Park and is operated by the Ohio Historical Society. For more information, contact Dunbar House State Memorial, 219 N. Paul Lawrence Dunbar Street, Box 1872, Dayton, 45401-1872, or call (513) 224-7061, or (800) 860-0148 or go to *www.ohiohistory.org/places/dunbar/*.

Zane Grey

No author better personifies a genre than Zane Grey. Although the western had been a literary form since the dime novels available in his youth, the genre reached its pinnacle in the adventure-packed fiction of Grey. His success enabled him to live an enviable lifestyle and gave an escape from the more mundane career of dentistry that originally seemed to be his fate.

He was born Pearl Zane Gray in 1872 in Zanesville, a city founded by his ancestors. As a boy, he loved fishing and baseball, but his strong-willed father had determined that his boy was to follow him in a dental career. He worked in his father's office before going off to the University of Pennsylvania on a baseball scholarship. He continued to play semi-pro baseball later, and a younger brother played briefly for the Pittsburgh Pirates in 1903.

After graduating from college, he moved to New York City to start his dental practice. But his practice foundered as he showed more interest in fishing and other outdoor activities. He also became interested in writing, submitting outdoor pieces and stories to various magazines. He had little success with this, possibly in part because he refused to use a typewriter and submitted his work in longhand. He did publish a novel in 1903 about his ancestor Betty Zane's heroism in the face of Indian attack, but had little success otherwise

His writing career received a boost when he married Lina "Dolly" Roth in 1905. His new wife offered encouragement and an inheritance, and the author now began to focus on the west for his material. He now began using his middle name and changed the spelling of his last name, and after years of hard work, Zane Grey became an overnight success. His first western, *Heritage in the Dust*, in 1910 was a success and by the time he wrote *Riders of the Purple Sage* in 1912, he was established as a master writer of the purple prose.

Leaving dentistry far behind, the Greys moved to Southern California, where Zane could also be near where many of his novels were made into movies. He traveled the world on hunting and fishing trips, and held several world fishing records. He wrote nearly 90 books before his death in 1939, and was the best-selling author of his era.

A replica of Zane Grey's study can be found at the National Road/Zane Grey Museum near his hometown. For further information, contact the National Road/ Zane Grey Museum, 8850 E. Pike, Norwich, 43767-9726 or call (740) 872-3143 or (800) 752-2602 or go to *www.ohiohistory.org/places/natroad.*

James Thurber

Although James Thurber is remembered as a sophisticated and urbane New York writer, he always carried with him the effects of his Columbus upbringing. He once observed that "the clocks that strike in my dreams are often the clocks of Columbus." He also featured characters and incidents from his hometown that personified a style that a *Time* magazine cover story referred to as having "a sure grasp of confusion."

James Thurber was born in Columbus in 1894 into an extended family of colorful eccentrics who later populated some of his funniest work. A childhood accident cost him one eye and eventually caused him to go completely blind. Despite this handicap, he did well at East High School and went on to attend Ohio State University. Here, the quieter Jamie became friends with Elliot Nugent, a student from Dover who helped steer him toward work on the school's paper and humor magazine. He left school during World War I to serve as a State Department code clerk in Paris.

After this service, Thurber returned home to work for the *Columbus Dispatch*, but he later returned to Paris as a correspondent for the *Chicago Tribune*. He was in Paris at the same time as other expatriate writers like Hemingway, Fitzgerald, and Louis Bromfield, but he did not stay long. He relocated to New York, where in 1927 he began a long association with a new magazine called *The New Yorker*.

Then, as now, The New Yorker was known for its cartoons, humor and short fiction- a perfect fit for Thurber, who excelled in all three categories. Not only did he become a part of the Algonquin Hotel-based circle of wits, but sharing an office with E.B. White, he refined his style and churned out a body of work that was collected into nearly 30 books. Thurber drew the illustrations for many of these. He also co-wrote a Broadway hit with Elliot Nugent, "The Male Animal", which was made into a movie. Masking his dark streak, Thurber's works often dealt with the war of the sexes and frequently offered fables with morals. He continued to regularly produce humorous prose until his death in 1961.

The house occupied by his family during Thurber's adolescence was restored in 1984. This is the residence featured in "The Night the Ghost Got In" and "The Night the Bed Fell," two of his more uproarious reminiscences. Today, the Thurber House serves both as museum and literary center, offering events and classes, a writer-in-residence program, and sponsors the prestigious Thurber Prize for American Humor. For more information, contact the Thurber House, 77 Jefferson Avenue, Columbus, 43215-3840 or call (614) 464-1032, or go to *www.thurberhouse.org.*

Louis Bromfield

Louis Bromfield's twin passions were writing and farming, and he proved he could excel at both. After winning a Pulitzer Prize for his earlier fiction, he spent his last years in his native Ohio advocating and demonstrating sound agricultural practices.

Bromfield was born in Mansfield in 1896. As a boy he enjoyed working on his grandfather's farm and as an adolescent he worked on a local newspaper. He originally went to college at Cornell to study agriculture but later switched to Columbia for journalism. But he quit college in World War I to serve as an ambulance driver assigned to the French Army.

After the war, he settled in New York City to seek a living as a writer. He found it in a surprisingly short time when his 1924 novel *The Green Bay Tree* became a critical and commercial success. Three years later he was awarded a Pulitzer Prize for his novel *Early Autumn* while he was barely 30 years old. By this time he had moved with his wife and daughters to France, where he continued to produce best sellers through 1938. Many of his books were also made into movies, which only increased his international prestige.

Yet in 1939 Bromfield gave up this lifestyle to return home. He purchased a 1,000-acre farm in his native Richland County, where he built a 32-room mansion called "the Big House" and turned them both into showcases. He devoted the rest of his life to conservation and progressive farm practices, and as a cultivated cultivator came to personify the Jeffersonian agrarian ideal. His later books, like *Pleasant Valley* and *Malabar Farm* were non-fiction works advocating simplicity and self-sufficiency.

While many noted Ohioans had to leave the state to become famous, Bromfield reversed this trend, and he actually brought Hollywood here. In 1945, the Big House was the scene of the wedding of Bromfield's friends Humphrey Bogart and Lauren Bacall in an effort to foil the paparazzi that stalk celebrity weddings. Bromfield wrote 30 books before his death in 1956, but his pioneering work in conservation practices may be his most lasting contribution. The Ohio Department of Agriculture headquarters is named for him.

This aspect is stressed at today's Malabar Farm, which became a state park in 1976. The park is now a working farm that features examples of all aspects of Ohio agriculture. It also offers tours of the Big House and a visitor education center that opened in 2006. In nearby Mansfield is Oak Hill Cottage, a home that is featured in the work of Bromfield. For more information about Malabar Farm, contact Malabar Farm State Park, 4050 Bromfield Road, Lucas, 44843 or call (419) 892-2784 or go to *www.malabarfarm.org*.

Sciences

Ohioans have also made major contributions in scientific and industrial fields. Charles Goodyear of Akron patented the process for vulcanizing rubber and made the tire industry possible, while Charles Kettering's invention of the automobile self-starter helped make the Dayton area an automotive manufacturing center. Thomas Edison, the most famous inventor of all, was born in the Erie County town of Milan. So diverse were his inventions and so wide-ranging their implications that aviation was one of the few areas he did not directly influence.

127

But several other Ohioans have more than picked up the slack in the realm of aviation. In addition to producing the inventors of the airplane and the first men to orbit the earth and land on the moon, Ohio also hosted the first air freight service, commercial crop dusting and national air races. Ohioans have played such a prominent role in the development of aviation that, in comparison, North Carolina's contribution seems limited to the hot air provided in the form of the warm breezes of Kitty Hawk.

A number of sites showcase Ohio's contribution to science and invention, and in particular to aviation.

Thomas Edison

Thomas Edison has become synonymous with invention. The holder of 1,093 patents, he was known as the Wizard of Menlo Park when he toiled night and day at his New Jersey laboratory. But he was a native of Ohio, born in Milan in 1847. He was the youngest of seven children, but the family did not stay long in Ohio. In 1854 they moved to Port Huron, Michigan, where Edison's father had found work as a lighthouse keeper. Although Edison never again resided in Ohio, he remained true to his roots and last visited his hometown in 1923 at age 76.

Edison's genius did not immediately manifest itself. He did not talk until he was four, and after just three months of school his teacher pronounced him "addled." Edison's mother then home schooled her now inquisitive son and encouraged him to pursue knowledge on his own. He thrived under this attention and his genius came to fruition as he increasingly learned from his own experimentation.

128

As a boy, Edison worked selling newspapers on the local railroad line, where two significant incidents affected him. A conductor trying to bring the boy onto the train grabbed him by the ears, which Edison claimed caused his hearing problems and eventual near-total deafness. In another incident, Edison saved a stationmaster's son from being hit by a train and was rewarded with telegraph lessons. This was no small gift, as telegraph operators were in short supply during the Civil War, and after mastering his new trade, Edison was able to find work wherever he went.

He came east to Boston and then relocated to New York in 1869. Here the ambitious and hard-working young man began to tinker with inventions. His first patent was for a stock ticker, and Edison found his new interests quite lucrative. Resolving to only invent things that people would buy, he set out also to control the production and distribution of his inventions. In many cases, he made marketable improvements to existing research, and with the proceeds he was able to open his research laboratory in Menlo Park in 1875.

Here he produced his most notable works, with the most celebrated being the electric light in 1879. After much trial and error experimentation, Edison was able to demonstrate a revolutionary invention that changed the world. Some of his other inventions also showed the connection between the worlds of art and science, as both the recording and film industries were made possible by his inventions of the phonograph and motion pictures. Edison became both wealthy and celebrated right up until his death in 1931.

Edison purchased the home where he was born in 1906 and on his last visit noted that the house was still not wired for electricity. That situation has been corrected, as the home is now a museum owned and operated by the Edison Birthplace Association. Located near the Milan Historical Museum, a seven building complex devoted to the same era, the Edison Museum features rare artifacts, tours and a gift shop. For more information, contact the Edison Birthplace Museum, 9 Edison Drive, Box 451, Milan, 44846-9739, or call (419) 499-2135 or go to *www.tomedison.org*.

The Wright Brothers

One does not have to look far to find examples of how Ohioans had the Wright stuff in pioneering aviation: the Wright family of Dayton produced the geniuses who gave flight to the world. Wilbur and Orrville Wright were the sons of Milton Wright, a bishop of the United Brethren of Christ Church. The boys also had a younger sister Katherine who played a major role in supporting them and their work. Their mother Susan was a tinkerer who encouraged their youthful experiments, but she became ill and died in 1889, while Orrville was still in high school.

His mother's illness and his own skating accident caused older brother Wilbur to cancel his plans to attend Yale, and Orrville soon dropped out of school and started a printing business in Dayton. The boys collaborated on a paper called the *West Side News* and published other projects. Tinkering with the machinery of the press led to other mechanical pursuits and in 1892 they started what became the Wright Cycle Company. They eventually started manufacturing and repairing bicycles, but by 1896 had already become fascinated with attempts to build a lighter than air flying machine.

They began to study this issue and corresponded with scientists in other countries who were attempting the same thing. A detailed study of weather data showed them that Kitty Hawk on the North Carolina coast offered literally the most favorable winds for success. The Wrights in 1900 began experimenting with engineless gliders in the breezes of Kitty Hawk, although they also built their own wind tunnel to better study the effects of air currents on flight. By 1903, they were ready to attempt a flight with a gasoline engine made by Charles Taylor, the master mechanic of the Wright Cycle Company.

On December 17 of that year they succeeded in Kitty Hawk breezes that were unusually cold. Orrville flew first in a flight that lasted twelve seconds and went only 120 feet, but on the last try of the day, Wilbur was in the air for 59 seconds and traveled 852 feet at an altitude of about ten feet. Despite their revolutionary success, much more work needed to be done. The next year, they resumed experimentation at Huffman Prairie in Dayton.

By 1905, the Wright brothers had improved their design and taught themselves to pilot well enough to present their creation to the world. Soon they became international celebrities and they traveled the world to promote their work and secure contracts. Katherine was included in the staging of flights and meeting of dignitaries. Bishop Wright even went on one flight at Huffman Prairie, which was the only day the boys flew together. They had promised their father they would not risk dying at the same time, which also would have deprived the world of considerable expertise.

With fame came conflict, and after 1909 much of the Wrights' time came to be taken up by patent related suits in the new airplane industry. Wilbur was more involved in this aspect, but he died of typhus in 1912 at age 45. Orrville sold his interest later and retired to his mansion at Hawthorne Hill, where he died in 1948. Neither brother ever married.

Dayton celebrates its aviation heritage today. A group called the Dayton Aviation Trail began preservation work that led in 1992 to the federal government establishing the Dayton Aviation Heritage National Historical Park. There are several sites around the city included under this banner. On Dayton's west side at Third and South Williams Streets, is the Wright-Dunbar Interpretive Center next door to the Wright Cycle Company. The features exhibits focus on the Wrights and their friend Paul Lawrence Dunbar, whose home is just a few blocks away (see page 120). At Carillon Historical Park, a 22 building, 65-acre museum dedicated to local history, is the original 1905 Wright Flyer. And Huffman Prairie, located near the U.S. Air Force Museum (see page 143), is open and has an interpretive center. The Air Force Museum also has a Wright Flyer on display. For more information, contact the Dayton Aviation Heritage National Historical Park, Box 9280, Wright Brothers Station, Dayton, 45409 or call (937) 228-7705 or go to *www.nps.gov/daav*.

Eddie Rickenbacker and Granville Woods

It's fortunate that Ohio has new museums opening all the time. Some of these new sites commemorate people or events that are in danger of being forgotten, while others bring to light stories that have never been properly told. An example that encompasses both of these is the Rickenbacker-Woods Technology Center, which preserves the memory of flying ace Eddie Rickenbacker and introduces Granville T. Woods—the Black Edison.

This new center is in the restored home of Rickenback-er, who lived here from 1895 until he married his wife

Adelaide in 1922. Rickenbacker was born in Columbus in 1890 to German speaking Swiss immigrants. His father died when Eddie was thirteen, and the boy quit school to help support the family. He had mechanical aptitude and a daring style and wound up becoming a racecar driver. He finished as high as tenth in the 1914 Indianapolis 500, but he left racing to join the service when America entered World War I.

Despite a lack of education and connections, Rickenbacker managed to get into the 94th Aero Squadron, America's first air combat unit. In just six months as a fighter pilot, he shot down 26 enemy aircraft, making him the top U.S. ace of the war. After the war, the returning hero started an automotive company that eventually failed. In 1925 he bought the Indianapolis Motor Speedway, and around the same time he began working with General Motors on both automotive and airplane engines.

Rickenbacker recognized the commercial as well as military implications for aviation, and in 1938 he became President of Eastern Airlines. This was the first airline to operate without any federal subsidiaries, and Rickenbacker continued to lead the company until his retirement in 1963. During World War II, he lent his experience to the military as an advisor and flew around the world. He had many close encounters with death, including survival of a 1941 plane wreck. But his closest brush with death came in 1942, when his military plane was blown off target and had to splash down in the Pacific when fuel ran out. He assumed leadership of eight survivors on a life raft as they drifted near Japanese territory for 24 days. Sustained by nothing but rainwater and fish and a bird that Rickenbacker caught, seven of eight men survived to be rescued. During the war, Rickenbacker also delivered a secret message to General MacArthur and traveled to Russia. A Medal of Honor winner, Rickenbacker was as deeply patriotic as he was technologically proficient, and he lived long enough to see men land on the moon.

Rickenbacker will now share his home with Granville Woods, who was born in Columbus in 1856. Educational opportunities for black students were limited at the time, and Woods had no schooling at all after the age of ten. He found work in a machine shop and discovered he was a quick learner with mechanical aptitude. He moved from job to job and learned from each one. He found work as a railroad fireman and advanced to become an engineer and got a job on a steam ship and rose to chief engineer.

However, a black man could only advance so high working for someone else, so Woods realized he was better off working for himself. He invented and sold the rights for a form of wireless telegraphy to Alexander Graham Bell and was able to start the Woods Electrical Company in Cincinnati. His company was involved in new advances in steam engine and electrical technology, and his stream of inventions earned him the nickname the Black Edison. His first patent was in 1889 for an improved steam boiler furnace and he had over 35 patents by the time he died in 1910.

The city of Columbus bought the Rickenbacker home in 1998 with the idea of turning it into a tribute to Rickenbacker and Woods. To further connect the aviator with the black inventor, the museum also intends to honor the Tuskegee Airman, the black WWII pilots who were based in Columbus after the war. For more information, contact the Rickenbacker-Woods Technology Center, 1334 Livingston Avenue, Columbus, 43204, or go to *www.columbusinfobase.org/RickWoods/RickWoodsHome.*

John Glenn

Ohio's strong impact upon aviation has continued into the space age. The state has produced 24 astronauts, with over half of them coming from the Cleveland area, which is also home to the NASA Glenn Visitor Center. While heavily populated New York and California have contributed more astronauts, Ohio ranks first in astronauts per capita. So predominant has been Ohio's role that in a 1995 mission of the Shuttle Discovery, four of five crew members were Ohioans. Governor George Voinovich solved this discrepancy by declaring the fifth astronaut as an honorary Buckeye.

Of all the Ohio astronauts, the first one is still the most famous. John Glenn personifies the Right Stuff that Tom Wolfe wrote of in his book on the first astronauts. Glenn was born in Cambridge in 1921 but his family moved to nearby New Concord when he was just two. He grew up along Main Street, which was also U.S. Route 40, the Main Street of America. Glenn's idyllic youth came to represent the best of small town virtue, and he even married his childhood sweetheart Anne Castor.

Both of them were graduates of Muskingum College, but after Pearl Harbor, John had entered the naval aviation cadet program. Upon graduating he was sent off to become a Marine fighter pilot. He flew 59 combat missions and rose to the rank of captain and stayed in the service after the war. After serving as a flight instructor, he was sent into combat again when the Korean War began. Here he flew 63 more missions, many alongside his fellow pilot baseball star Ted Williams.

After the Korean War, Glenn became a test pilot. In 1957, he made the first supersonic transcontinental flight, and when NASA started the space program he and six others were picked over 500 applicants to become America's first astronauts. He was the third American to go up into space but the first to orbit the earth on February 20, 1962. Five years after setting a record by flying across the country in three and a half hours, he went around the earth three times in less than five hours.

Glenn's trip made him a national hero and he was given a ticker tape parade in New York. In 1964 he retired from the service as a colonel and entered politics. He would up serving Ohio for 24 years in the U.S. Senate and also ran for the Presidency in 1984. In 1998, at age 77 he went up in space again—36 years after his previous flight. His second flight offered a chance to study space geriatrics, a fitting end to his Senatorial career that led to a second New York City ticker tape parade.

Glenn's boyhood home is now preserved as the John and Annie Glenn Historical Site. Glenn was reluctant to endorse the project originally but agreed if the educational aspects were stressed. The emphasis is on the local interaction with the 20th Century as seen by members of the household. For more information, contact The John and Annie Glenn Historic Site, 72 West Main Street, Box 107, New Concord, 43762 or call (740) 826-3305 or go to *www.johnglennhome.org.*

Neil Armstrong

The culmination of aviation events of the 20th Century occurred when the U.S. successfully put men on the moon in 1969. And once again, it was an Ohioan who made the giant leap. Neil Armstrong was born in Auglaize County in 1930, the oldest child of rural parents. They moved to Wapakoneta when Neil was thirteen, and here he became an Eagle Scout and graduated from high school. He went to Purdue University to study aeronautical engineering, but was drafted in 1949.

In the service he trained intensively to become a Naval Aviator and learned how to land on the deck of an aircraft carrier. He was sent to Korea in August of 1951 and just five days later his plane was shot down, although he was able to safely eject. Armstrong flew 78 missions in Korea and left the service as a Lieutenant in 1952. Returning to Purdue, he met his wife Janet, who he married after graduating in 1955.

After moving to California, Armstrong became a test pilot for NASA and also eventually got a Master's in Aeronautical Engineering from the University of Southern California. As an experimental pilot, Armstrong was involved in flying the new X-15 rockets and he also flew with flying legend Chuck Yeager. In 1962, Armstrong joined the astronaut program, and four years later went into space as commander of the Gemini 8 mission, which involved the docking of space vehicles.

This helped prepare him for his role as commander of the Apollo 11 mission and the first moon landing. On July 20, 1969, Armstrong set foot on the moon with the words, "That's one small step for a man, one giant leap for mankind." It had been over a thousand years since the ancient Hopewells had lined up the moonrise over Ohio fields. But it was only 65 years after the Wright brothers worked out the bugs of flight in Dayton that an Ohioan set foot on the moon. Armstrong left the space program the next year, but he avoided the limelight rather than capitalize on his fame. He was a professor at the University of Cincinnati until 1979 and he worked in the private sector after that. He did not even consent to a biography until 2005.

The Neil Armstrong Air and Space Museum reflects the modesty of its namesake. Although displays feature a glamorous test plane and the Gemini 8 capsule, the focus is on all Ohioans who contributed to space flight. For more information, contact the Armstrong Air and Space Museum, Box 1978, 500 S. Apollo Drive, Wapakoneta, 45895-1978 or call (419) 738-8811 or (800) 860-0142 or go to *www.ohiohistory.org/places/Armstrong.*

Chapter Seven:
Other Categories

There are many other worthwhile Ohio historical sites that can be arranged in various categories. For example, many sites are devoted to the roles that various forms of transportation played in Ohio's status as a national crossroads. There is also an abundance of preserved or rebuilt villages that offer history buffs the opportunity to see first-hand how life was lived at various periods of the state's history. In addition, there are several homes open to the public that showcase the lifestyles of individual families of different periods. A trio of outdoor dramas tell dramatic tales from pioneer times in Ohio. And finally, there are many fine museums devoted to both general and specific subjects that may not fit into previously discussed categories, but are worthy of a visit. Here is a limited sample of some Ohio sites that may not fit themes of previous chapters, yet should be mentioned.

Transportation

Ohio has played a major role in transportation history beyond its role in the development of air travel. The southern border of the Ohio River served as both an east-west highway and a north-south boundary in the nation's early history. The northern border of Lake Erie and Canada placed Ohio between two major water routes and guaranteed the state a permanent role in water travel. Connecting these bodies was an elaborate canal system, and the Muskingum River lock and dam system that today uses the same hand powered locks as in the 1840's. The first national road passed through the middle of Ohio and the state was also home to some of the earlier efforts in railroad travel in the 19th century that resulted in Ohio having the largest interurban system in the country. In the 20th century, both the automotive and aviation industries had roots here. There are a number of museums that showcase Ohio's role in transportation history, and here are some of them,

Ohio River Museum, 601 Second Street, Marietta, 45750-2122. (740) 373-3750, or (800) 860-0145. *www.ohiohistory.org/places/ohioriver.* Operated by the Ohio Historical Society in conjunction with the Campus Martius Museum, which specializes in migration to Ohio and is just a block away. Commemorates steamboat and river commerce and includes tours of the W.P. Snyder, the last steam-powered, stern wheeled towboat in the U.S.

National Road/Zane Grey Museum, 8850 East Pike, Norwich, 43767. (740) 872-3143, or (800) 752-2602. *www.ohiohistory.org/places/natlroad.* The first federal interstate highway is celebrated here with extensive dioramas showing the development of America's Main Street. Also houses the Zane Grey Museum (see page 121).

Lockington Locks, Lockington. Features remains of Miami and Erie Canal locks. Part of the Piqua Historical Area. 9845 North Hardin Road, Piqua, 45356. (937) 773-2522,or(800) 752-2619. *www.ohiohistory.org.places/locking.* Piqua Historical Area also offers rides on the General Harrison of Piqua, a mule-drawn canal boat.

Inland Seas Maritime Museum of the Great Lakes Historical Society, 480 Main Street, Vermillion 44089-0435. (440) 967-3467 or (800) 893-1485. *www.inlandseas.org.* Features shipwreck artifacts, models on display and hands-on exhibits.

Fairport Marine Museum and Lighthouse, 129 Second Street, Fairport Harbor, 44077-5816. (440) 354-4825. *www.neweb.com/org/fhlh.* A museum that features a tour of an 1871 lighthouse, one of eleven Ohio lighthouses on Lake Erie's shore.

Ashtabula Marine Museum, 1071 Walnut Blvd., Box 2804, Ashtabula, 44005-2804. (440) 224-0972. *www.ashtabulamarinemuseum.org.* A nautical heritage museum in the former lighthouse keeper's residence.

Western Lake Erie Historical Society, *S.S. Willis Boyer* Museum Ship, 26 Main Street, Box 5311, Toledo. (419) 936-3070. *www.internatioalpark.org.* Features a tour of a 617-foot long freighter built in 1911.

Mad River and NKP Railroad Museum, 233 York Street, Bellevue, 49811-1377 (Museum located at 253 SouthwestStreet).(419)483-2222. *www.madrivermuseum.org.* Features vintage cars and artifacts from the heyday of railroads.

Dennison Railroad Depot Museum, 400 Center Street, Box 11, Dennison, 44621-0011. (740) 922-6776. *www.dennisondepot.org.* Museum in 1873 depot also celebrates Dennison canteen, which fed troop trains during World War II.

Ohio Railway Museum, Box 777, 900 Proprietors Road, Worthington, 44085. (614) 885-7345. *www.ohiorailwaymuseum.org.* Recently opted to specialize in trolleys, interurbans and streetcars.

Canton Classic Car Museum, Market Avenue at 6th Street SW, Canton, 44702. (330) 455-3603. *www.cantonclassiccar.org.* Features autos and memorabilia from the 1920s through the 1970s.

United States Air Force Museum, 1100 Spaatz Street, Wright-Patterson AFB, 45433-7102. (937) 255-3286. *www.wpafb.af.mil.museum.* Features over ten acres of exhibits, 300 aircraft and an IMAX theatre.

Another transportation-related area where Ohio plays a prominent role is covered bridges. There are fewer than 1,000 of these relics left nationally, but Ohio ranks third in number of covered bridges still standing. These bridges can be found throughout Ohio, with numerous good examples found in Ashtabula, Fairfield, Preble and Washington counties.

Another nostalgic reminder of a bygone era, the Mail Pouch barn, is still seen frequently in southeastern Ohio. Harley Warrick, the last of the Mail Pouch painters, lived in Belmont County, and before his death in 2002, he passed on some tips to Scott Hagan of neighboring Monroe County. Hagan then painted the Ohio Bicentennial logo on barns in all 88 Ohio counties.

Villages and Farms

Ohio is blessed with numerous preserved or rebuilt villages and farms that depict how life was lived in various eras. These sites are scattered throughout the state and represent all periods of Ohio history. All of them offer something unique for the historic traveler.

Sun Watch Indian Village and Archeological Park, 2301 West River Road, Dayton, 45418. (937) 268-8199. *www.sunwatch.org*. Rebuilt homes and gardens show how the Fort Ancient Indians lived 800 years ago,

Schoenbrunn State Memorial, Box 129, State Route 259, New Philadelphia, 44663-0129. (330) 339-3636, or (800) 752-2711. *www.ohiohistory.org/places/schoenbr*. Features eighteen rebuilt log buildings from a 1772 village built by Christian Delaware Indians and the Moravian missionaries who converted them.

Roscoe Village 381 Hill Street, located along Whitewoman Street, Coshocton, 43812-1098. (800) 877-1830, or (740) 622-9310. *www.roscoevillage.com.* Restored town that shows life in the 1830s, along the Ohio and Erie Canal.

Zoar Village State Memorial, Box 404, Zoar, 44697-0404. (330) 874-4336, or (800) 874-4336. *www.zcq.org.* German Separatists founded this communal village in 1817 and many original buildings remain.

Historic Lyme Village, Box 342, 5487 St. Rt. 113, Bellevue, 44811-0342.(419)483-4949. *www.lymevillage.com.* A collection of buildings covering the 19th century, including a farmhouse that was a stop on the Underground Railroad.

Hale Farm and Village, Box 296, 2686 Oak Hill Rd., Bath, 44210-0296. (330)666-3711. *www.wrhs.org/halefarm.* Focuses on artisans and craftsmen of the early 19th century,

Caeser's Creek Pioneer Village, Box 1049, Waynesville,45068.(513)897-6546. *www.caeserscreekvillage.org.* Has thirty buildings from the first half of the 19th Century relocated on a green,

Au Glaize Village and Farm Museum, Box 801, 12296 Krouse Road, Defiance, 43512. (419) 784-0107, or (419) 782-7255. *www.defiance-online.com/auglaize.* Depicts rural life in the 1800s.

Sauder Farm and Craft Village, Box 235, 22611 State Route 2, Archbold, 43502. (800) 590-9755. *www.saudervillage.org*. A large complex stressing rural life and crafts from the 19th century,

Ohio Village, Ohio Historical Society, 1982 Velma Avenue, Columbus, 43211-2497. (614) 297-2300, or (800) 686-1124. *www.ohiohistory.org*. A Civil War era village that is now open for special events only.

Stongsville Historical Village, 13305 Pearl Road, Strongsville, 44136-3403. (216) 572-0557. Contains buildings from between 1816 and 1904.

Wolcott Museum Complex, 1031 River Rd., Maumee, 43537-3460. Call this number for information, (419) 893-9602. *www.maumee.org/recreation/wolcott.htm*. Contains four homes, a train depot and a church.

Burton Century Village, Box 153, 14653 E. Park Street, Burton, 44021-0153. (440) 834-4012. *www.burtonchamberofcommerce.org.* Contains twenty buildings centered around downtown.

Bob Evans Farm and Homestead Museum, Box 198, or Canoe Livery Road, Rio Grande, 45674. (740) 245-5305, or (800) 994-3276. *www.bobevans.com.* Celebrates not only the history of the company but Ohio's rural heritage,

Slate Run Living Historical Farm, 1375 State Route 674 North, Canal Winchester, 43110. (614) 833-1880. *www.metroparks.net/parksslaterun/aspx.* A working farm from the 1880s.

Carriage Hill Metro Farm Park, 7800 E. Shull Rod, Dayton,45424-1535. Call this number for information (513) 879-0461. *www.dayton.net/audubon/carghl.html.* An 1880s farm with visitor's center.

Most of these sites host festivals or special events that focus on their particular era. There are many other regular festivals that celebrate crafts and history, such as the Salt Fork Arts and Crafts Festival in Guernsey County and the Algonquin Mills Festivals in Carroll County. These shows range in size from the large Fair at New Boston in Clark County, and the Yankee Peddler Festival in Stark County to the more intimate Soakum Festival in Noble County. For more information on Ohio historical festivals, contact the Ohio Festivals and Events Association at *www.ofea.org.*

147

Homes

Homes that have been turned into museums are all over Ohio. Nearly every local historical society has one, or plans to, and all are worth a visit. Some of these homes typify the lifestyle of a particular locale or period, while others have connections with fascinating people. Here are just a few examples of historic homes now available for public touring. Many of them also offer special events such as Christmas tours.

Loghurst Farm Museum, 3967 Boardman-Canfield Road, Canfield, 44406-9030. (330)533-4330. *www.wrhs.org*. Built in 1806 and believed to be the oldest log home in the Western Reserve, this farmhouse was also a stop on the Underground Railroad.

Adena State Memorial, Box 831, Adena Road, Chillicothe, 45601. (740) 772-1500, or (800) 319-7248. *www.ohiohistory.org/places/adena.* This 1807 stone mansion was the home of Thomas Worthington, "the father of Ohio statehood."

John Johnston Home, Piqua Historical Area, 9845 North Hardin Road, Piqua, 45356. (937) 773-2522, or (800) 752-2619. *www.ohiohistory.org/places/piqua/.* The restored 1820's home (see photo) of a farmer canal commissioner and Indian agent shares the grounds with the Eastern Woodland Indian museum the canal boat General Harrison of Piqua., and the site of Fort Pickawillany.

The Castle, 418 Fourth Street, Marietta, 45750. (740) 373-4180. *www.mariettacastle.org.* An 1855 Gothic Revival Mansion that hosts educational programs and special events.

Piatt Castles, Box 497, 10051 Township Road 47, West Liberty, 43357. (937) 465-2821.*www.piattcastles.org.* Two stone manors that have been open for tours for 100 years.

Benninghofen House Museum, 327 N. Second Street, Hamilton, 45011-1651. (513) 896-9930. *www.home.fuse.net/butlercountymuseum.* Italianate home of Gilded Age, industrialist.

J. E. Reeves Victorian Home and Carriage House Museum, 325 E. Iron Ave., Dover, 44622. (330) 343-7040, or (800) 815-2794.*www.doverhistory.org.* Restored seventeen-room 1900 mansion of industrialist and banker.

Stan Hywet Hall and Gardens, 714 North Portage Path, Akron, 44303-1399. (330) 836-5533, or (888) 836-5533.

149

www.stanhywet.org. This 1912 home of Goodyear co-founder F.S. Seiberling features a 70-acre landscaped grounds as well as a 65-room Tudor mansion.

The Westcott House, 1340 East High Street, Springfield, 45505. (937) 327-9291. *www.westcotthouse.org.* Recently renovated Prairie-style home designed by Frank Lloyd Wright.

Outdoor Dramas

Completely different from home tours are outdoor dramas. They are different not only because they are outdoors, but also because they are less common and tend to focus on a specific era. The three longest-running outdoor dramas in Ohio each summer all deal with the period of white and Indian interaction on the frontier. These plays have all made alterations to history for dramatic purposes, but they illustrate in a spectacular way the conflicts of the period and offer material for discussion.

"Tecumseh" focuses on the life of the great Ohio-born Shawnee chief. It is presented at the Sugarloaf Mountain Amphitheatre near Chillicothe. For more information, call (740) 775-0700, or (866) 775-0700, or go to *www.tecumsehdrama.com.*

"Trumpet in the Land" tells the tragic story of Moravian missionaries and converted Delaware Indians during the American Revolution. It is shown at the Schoenbrunn Amphitheatre near New Philadelphia. For information, call (330) 339-1132, or go to *www.trumpetintheland.com.*

"Blue Jacket" poses the theory that a Shawnee war chief was actually a white man adopted into the tribe. It is offered at Caeser's Ford Park Amphitheatre near Xenia. To learn more, call (937) 376-4318, or (877) 465-2583, or go to *www.bluejacketdrama.com.*

Other Museums

There are some Ohio museums that are just too significant to be left out even if they don't fit neatly into the categories of this book. Some of them are strong general museums in metro areas, while others address specific subjects and have national appeal.

Ohio Historical Society, 1982 Velma Avenue, Columbus, 43211-2497. (614) 297-2300, or (800) 686-6124. *www.ohiohistory.org.* Offers a research facility in addition to a comprehensive museum devoted to the state's history.

Cincinnati History Museum, part of Cincinnati Museum Center at Union Terminal, 1301 Western Avenue, Cincinnati, 45203. (513) 287-7000, or (800) 733-2077. *www.cincymuseum.org.* Part of a major complex centered in the city's distinctive 1933 art deco railroad terminal.

Western Reserve Historical Society Museum, 10825 East Blvd., Cleveland, 44106. (216) 721-5722. *www.wrhs.org.* Located in the culturally rich University Circle area, near art museum and museum of natural history.

Historical Center of Industry and Labor, Box 573, 151 West Wood Street, Youngstown, 44501. (330) 743-5934,or (800)262-6137. *www.ohiohistory.org/places/youngst.* Documents the rise and fall of the steel industry in the Mahoning Valley.

Pro Football Hall of Fame, 2121 George Halas Drive N.W., Canton, 44708. (330) 456-8207. *www.profootballhof.com.* A popular attraction with national appeal.

Rock and Roll Hall of Fame and Museum, One Key Plaza, Cleveland, 44114. (888) 764-7625. *www.rockhall.com.* Features 150,000 square feet of exhibit space in a unique new building.

Motts Military Museum, 5075 South Hamilton Road, Groveport, 43125. (614)836-1500. *www.mottsmilitarymuseum.org.* Collects memorabilia and stories pertaining to U.S. military history.

152

These are just a few of the better-known museums in the state. There are many other sites specializing in such diverse subjects as dentistry, firefighting, trapshooting, paperweights, ceramics and postal history. In addition, there are numerous local historical societies all across the state that all have something unique to offer. Visit as many of these as you can.

For Further Reading

Altoff, Gerald T. *Oliver Hazard Perry and the Battle of Lake Erie*. Put-in-Bay, OH: The Perry Group, 1999.

Cash, James B. *Unsung Heroes: Ohioans in the White House: A Modern Appraisal*. Wilmington, OH: Orange Frazer Press, 1998.

Booth, Stephane Elise. *Buckeye Women*. Athens: Ohio University Press, 2001.

Friends of Freedom Society. *Freedom Seekers: Ohio and the Underground Railroad*. Columbus: Friends of Freedom Press, 2004.

Gorczyca, Beth. *Ohio's Bicentennial Barns*. Wooster, OH: Wooster Book Co., 2003.

Garrison, Webb. *A Treasury of Ohio Tales: Unusual, Interesting and Little Known Stories of Ohio*. Nashville, TN: Rutledge Hill Press, 1993.

Horwitz, Lester V. *The Longest Raid of the Civil War*. Cincinnati: Farmcourt Publishing, 1999.

Knepper, George W. *Ohio and Its People*. Kent, OH: Kent

State University Press, 2003.

Lepper, Bradley T. *Ohio Archeology: An Illustrated Chronicle of Ohio's Ancient American Indian Cultures.* Wilmington, OH: Orange Frazer Press.

Parker, John P. ed. By Stuart Seely Sprague. *His Promised Land: The Autobiography of John P. Parker.* New York: W.W. Norton, 1996.

Siebert, Wilbur H. *The Mysteries of Ohio's Underground Railroad.* Columbus: Long's College Book Co., 1951.

Sowash, Rick. *Heroes of Ohio: 23 True Tales of Courage and Character.* Bowling Green: Gabriel's Horn Publishing, 1998.

Weeks, Philips, ed. *Buckeye Presidents: Ohioans in the White House.* Kent, OH: Kent State University Press, 2003.

Williams, Gary S. *The Forts of Ohio: A Guide to Military Stockades.* Caldwell, OH: Buckeye Book Press, 2003.

Williams, Gary S. *Spies, Scoundrels and Rogues of the Ohio Frontier.* Caldwell, OH: Buckeye Books Press, 2005.

Woods, Miriam. *The Covered Bridges of Ohio: An Atlas and History.* Columbus: Old Trail Printing, 1993.

Woodward, Susan L. and Jerry N. McDonald. *Indian Mounds of the Middle Ohio Valley.* Blacksburg, VA: McDonald and Woodward Publishing Company, 2002.

Index of Sites by County
With page number for contact information

157

About The Author

Gary S. Williams is a lifelong resident of Ohio. A native of Tuscarawas County, his first job was on the archaeological excavation of Fort Laurens, Ohio's only Revolutionary War fort. He has a B.A. in History from Marietta College, a Masters of Library Science from Kent State University, and 25 years experience as a librarian. He lives near Caldwell with his wife Mary. This is his fourth book.

Please direct correspondence, speaking requests and book requests to:

Gary S. Williams
42100 Williams Lane
Caldwell, OH 43724
Phone: (740) 732-8169 or (740) 732-7291
Email: buckeye_books@earthlink.net
Website: www.buckeyebookpress.com

Also Available From Buckeye Book Press

The Forts of Ohio: A Guide to Military Stockades

The earliest years of Ohio's recorded history were filled with conflict as Americans, Europeans and Native Americas struggled for control of the region. For the white intruders of this era, log forts became the key to survival in this wilderness. The story of these forts is the story of Ohio's beginnings and features some compelling tales. At which Ohio fort...

- did one of that nation's most famous friendship begin when Lewis met Clark?
- did the officers write a Declaration of Independence that preceded the more famous one by 20 months?
- was a future President arrested for ordering that a civilian be given 50 lashes?
- did the besieged and starving garrison stampede their own relief convoy by firing guns in celebration?
- was an American general, who was also a spy for Spain, suspected of trying to kill Anthony Wayne?
- did the commander name the post after his eleven-year-old daughter?
- did Tecumseh complain that the Americans "hide behind logs and in the earth like ground hogs"?
- did Commodore Perry send his famous message, "We have met the enemy and they are ours?"

163

Also Available From Buckeye Book Press

Spies, Scoundrels and Rogues of the Ohio Frontier

Though thoroughly American today, the region between the Great Lakes and the states bordering the Ohio River was once rife with international intrigue. Between 1754 and 1814 several nations and tribes competed for this resource-rich region, and the interplay between them produced a colorful cast of less than reputable characters. Among the examples profiled here are:

- a famous soldier and author who failed in his attempt to create a transcontinental empire and died in disgrace
- a Tory spy who originally impressed George Washington but wound up alienating everyone with his lies and bullying
- the most famous and most hated of renegade traitors
- two ill-suited officers who led Americans into massacres
- a popular folk legend who lived to kill Indians
- the most notorious organized crime figure of the frontier
- an Indian Agent who betrayed Indians and whites alike in both times of peace and war; yet died a hero's death
- the only one of the Burr Conspirators to escape unscathed, although he was more guilty than any of them

The subjects range chronologically from the accused traitors Robert Rogers to Aaron Burr, and in public estimation from Lewis Wetzel to Simon Girty, and their behavior collectively tells the story of this fascinating era.

164